TH
SWELLING SCENE

The development of amateur drama in Hull from 1900

Compiled by

Pamela Dellar and Gillian Holtby

and edited by

Barbara Robinson

Introduction by **Alan Plater**

Highgate of Beverley

Highgate Publications (Beverley) Limited
1996

DEDICATION

THIS BOOK is dedicated in affection and gratitude to the memory of Stella Sizer-Simpson and Peter S. Harvey, whose Janus Theatre was only one of their many contributions to the dramatic arts.

> *But we were young then, and 'the play was the thing . . .'*

ACKNOWLEDGMENTS

THE EDITOR and the compilers wish to thank all the amateur theatre enthusiasts and workers who have contributed to this book and to the "swelling scene" of theatre in Hull during the 20th century.

Our special thanks to Mollie Goodare and the amateur drama secretaries who kindly responded to our questionnaire; also to John Markham of Highgate Publications and Barry Sage of BA Print.

THE TITLE, *The Swelling Scene,* is from the Prologue of Shakespeare's *Henry V.*

THE COVER DESIGN has been adapted by Simon Robinson from Louise Jacobs' souvenir programme for the Hull Little Theatre, 1926-27.

British Library Cataloguing in Publication Data.
A catalogue record for this book is available from the British Library.

© 1996 Barbara Robinson

ISBN 0 948929 93 6

Published by

Highgate of Beverley

Highgate Publications (Beverley) Limited
24 Wylies Road, Beverley, HU17 7AP
Telephone (01482) 866826

Produced by

ba/*print*

4 Newbegin, Lairgate, Beverley, HU17 8EG
Telephone (01482) 886017

CONTENTS

Souvenir for 1914

INTRODUCTION

By Alan Plater

MY FIRST THEATRICAL MEMORY is of Sandy Powell saying, 'Can you hear me, Mother?' from the stage of the Palace Theatre in Hull. The family had moved to the City from Jarrow-on-Tyne in 1938 and the variety bill in question must have been in that year, or early in 1939. During that same period we also saw Harry Roy and his band and the celebrated organist, Reginald Foort. Theatre organists were the rock stars of the day. It is a long time ago.

The first Shakespearean production I saw was at the New Theatre in or around 1952 – an Old Vic production of *Othello* with Douglas Campbell. Memory – which is a very slippery customer in these matters – tells me a gang of us went to the New on a Saturday night, and to hear the Humphrey Lyttleton Band at the City Hall on the Sunday.

A zealous researcher trawling through the archives might well prove that memory is telling me a pack of lies, but the images that linger are so powerful that they will serve as truth; and, like all the best stories, they have sequels waiting around the corner. I had the good fortune to grow up into a professional writer, and to work with Douglas Campbell in the theatre, and with Sandy Powell on a BBC TV documentary about the history of the seaside, transmitted in 1974, if my own archive is to be believed.

We shot the film in Brighton, where Sandy was playing a summer season with Elsie and Doris Waters, Nat Jackley, Bob and Alf Pearson and Leslie Sarony. What larks! Every day I took a stroll around the history of British music-hall, and every evening I contrived to be in the theatre for Sandy's act. He was a gentle, beguiling performer, confirming the ancient truth: if you want people to listen to you, speak quietly. He also honoured the golden rule of stand-up comedy: make sure your opening line is a good one. He was then in his mid-70s, though he shed 20 years the minute he walked on stage. He made his entrance and said, 'I know what you're all thinking. (Pause) Is he still alive?'

Another ancient truth: we are all readers before we are writers, and we are all theatre-goers before we are playwrights. During the formative years, my theatre-going tended to be split between the so-called 'popular' and the 'legitimate' – the former category embracing such as Norman Evans, the great Max Wall, and the comedians' comedian, Jimmy James, in whose honour I called my most recent play, *I Thought I Heard a Rustling* – a quotation from his famous lions-in-the-box routine – and a range of marvellous eccentric performers. Does anyone else remember Herschel Henlere, comedy pianist, or Doctor Crock and his Crackpots? And even I have forgotten the name of the double-act who specialised in playing xylophones while on roller-skates.

Parallel with these joyful evenings at the Tivoli and Palace, I was also learning about proper grown-up drama at the New, either in touring versions or presented by the Salberg Repertory Company, who used to boast about their popularity, quoting attendance figures in their *Hull Daily Mail* ads. Among the touring productions, I recall Ralph Richardson in Robert Bolt's *Flowering Cherry* and a revue written by Keith Waterhouse and Willis Hall, *England our England*, with, among others, the wonderful and much-lamented Roy Kinnear. Again, destiny was lurking: I ended up working with Roy, have watched Rugby League Cup Finals with Willis Hall and had the same agent as Bob Bolt – the entirely remarkable Peggy Ramsay. For the record, I also worked with a jazz pianist who, early in his career, played occasional dates with Doctor Crock. Apparently the band rehearsals took the form of a brief chat in the pub before the show.

In terms of my theatrical education, the Salberg Players have a deal to answer for too. In retrospect, their policy seems to have been more adventurous than the average. I certainly remember seeing Peter Ustinov's *Love of Four Colonels* when it felt like the sharp end of the avant-garde. Then, on the cusp of the 50s and 60s, I saw John Osborne's *Look Back in Anger* and Arnold Wesker's *Roots*, both at the New, though, hand on heart, I cannot remember any details of the productions. But something akin to a revolution was taking place, and, like any self-respecting young man, I started to cultivate my anger.

So far I have only listed enthusiasms; but as the years passed by, discrimination crept into my psyche. This generally took the form of questions. Why was that play so tedious? Why did it take 20 minutes to get started? How could the police inspector be so stupid? Why are these people drinking gin and tonic all the time? Who cares what happens in this drawing room in the Home Counties? And where are the Home Counties anyway? Like Alan Bleasdale's Yosser Hughes, I was saying, 'I could do that', albeit less publicly and aggressively. Shakespeare's status was not under any threat but I calculated I could match some of the thrillers that failed to thrill and the comedies that failed to amuse.

There were two other elements in the equation. Wesker and Co. had proved that plays were not obliged to take place in a drawing-room in the Home Counties. Drama, like life, could happen anywhere. To this I added my own personal and continuing obsession, an attempt to fuse the 'popular' and the 'legitimate'. Why should theatre be the exclusive preserve of people with a house full of O and A levels? This, of course, was not an original observation, but these things cannot be taught – they have to be learned, slowly and at your own chosen speed.

My first plays were written for radio and television, in that golden age when there were 300 original plays on our screens every year. Some of them were terrible, mine included, but it was a fine apprenticeship. As Frank Muir and/or Dennis Norden once said, 'What a new writer needs is a place to be lousy in.'

These plays served as a springboard into the theatre. My first professional production was a double-bill at the Victoria Theatre, Stoke-on-Trent, in 1963. Its director, Peter Cheeseman, had a personal company of six, including a young chap called Alan Ayckbourn. The theatre was housed in a converted cinema and the heating didn't work. The first night took place in the middle of a blizzard to an audience of four paying customers and 20 assorted friends on complimentary tickets. The Western European Theatre did not tilt on its axis.

The 1960s, whatever our former Prime Minister says, were a remarkable decade, if only because the Performing Arts were not sneered at. I wrote my first full-length stage play for The Victoria, and others for the Library Theatre in Scarborough, the Newcastle Playhouse and the Harrogate Festival. But another thought was beginning to nag, especially when driving back and forth on the Stoke Road, such as it was, in an unheated Standard Eight without a windscreen washer. The thought was this: if Stoke (Pop. 262,000), Newcastle (Pop. 217,000) and Harrogate (Pop. 64,000) thought it worthwhile to have a professional producing theatre, what was wrong with Hull (Pop. 282,000)? The statistics are based on 1972 figures, but the point is clear enough.

The City of Hull had given me a formal and a theatrical education and much of my writing was based on a life lived in the City – but we had no permanent professional acting company. To their eternal credit, the amateurs had made me welcome – notably the Company of the Way and the Garret Players – but they, too, felt the need for a proper professional focus for everyone's work. Like all good democrats, we formed a committee. The story of the making of the Hull Arts Centre, which begat Humberside Theatre, which begat Spring Street Theatre, now Hull Truck Theatre, is told elsewhere in this book, but let me offer a pre-emptive footnote:

During our campaigning period, we described our aims as the creation of 'a workshop and a shop window' for artists of all kinds. Twenty years on, it is possible to catalogue some of the people who used Spring Street for exactly those purposes: Anthony Minghella, Jim Hawkins, Phil Woods, Brian Clark, Harry Duffin, Barry Hanson, Frances Barber, Bob Hoskins, Richard Beckinsale, Frances Tomelty, Mike Bradwell, David Threlfall, Jon Marshall and, more recently, John Godber. These names are, once more, from memory; a couple of hours in the files would reveal ten times as many. It is, by any standards, an impressive list and this is the moment to say, loudly and clearly, we were right and the sceptics were wrong.

The constant factor throughout all these stories is the City of Hull. It is, to be sure, a strange, wondrous, exasperating place, its isolation breeding, at best, a sturdy independence of spirit, at worst, an introspective parochialism. What the City needs, now as it did in the 1960s, is a transplant of Liverpool brashness and Geordie passion. In cultural as well as sporting terms, the City should always be in the First Division. The lesson of this book is that 'theatrically' Hull has enjoyed major league status more often than is generally supposed. The challenge, as ever and always, is to make that position permanent.

Alan Plater.

THE HULL PLAYGOERS

By Margaret Burnett

WHEN TRACING the history of the amateur theatre, we find that the Hull Playgoers' Society played a large part in the development of the New Theatre. In 1901, Duce Mohamed, a well-known Arabian living in the area, had much to do with the founding of the Hull Shakespeare Society. Mr Mohamed had a deep interest in, and knowledge of, Shakespeare's plays, and was an excellent speaker of verse. Members met regularly in the Assembly Rooms in Kingston Square, and devoted their time to the study and reading of the plays.

After a time, like all amateur – and, indeed, professional – companies, they came up against financial troubles. Then, however, the Society's president, Tom Sheppard, teamed up with Holbrook Jackson, who was trying to form a Playgoers' Society in Hull on the same lines as those in Leeds and other large towns. To avoid having two societies vying with each other to keep alive, they decided to join forces, and the result was the Hull Shakespeare and Playgoers' Society, launched in 1921.

Meetings were held in a studio in the Assembly Rooms, which are now the New Theatre as we know it. Shakespeare was still a priority, and on 23 April 1922 – Shakespeare was born on 23 April, 1564 – members met in the Banqueting Hall there to hear a lecture on the Bard by Henry Baynton, a young Shakespearean actor who was appearing in *The Merchant of Venice* at the Alexandra Theatre in George Street, sadly no longer in existence. At that time there was a close link between the amateurs and the professionals.

In 1924, Edgar Appleton, then a leading figure in the amateur world, who later worked frequently in the professional theatre, proposed that the name of the society be changed to Hull Playgoers' Society, a more manageable title, and it is still thriving today under that name. Its objects were, and indeed still are, to quote from Tom Sheppard, 'To stimulate interest in the whole art of the theatre and enable its members, by readings, discussions, lectures and performances, to become acquainted with the best in modern and classical drama'.

Repertory

In 1924, the repertory movement took off in this country, and our neighbours beat us to it. Leeds had its own Arts Theatre, where local dramatic talent, whether through actor or author, shared with the professional in the recognition and encouragement of its merits. It was the same in York, with its Everyman Theatre.

In August 1924, the actor and director, Arthur R. Whatmore, was preparing to bring his repertory season to the Little Theatre in Jarratt Street, next door to the Assembly Rooms, and here he opened on 13 September 1924. As in other repertory theatres, Whatmore enlisted the help of local actors and actresses, stage-managers and electricians – and Hull Playgoers and the Hull amateur operatic societies were well to the fore. Finance always created a hurdle which had to be surmounted. The Little Theatre provided three or four seasons of 'rep' each year, and in between Hull Playgoers put on several productions to keep the theatre alive.

The first of their performances was *Aucassin and Nicolette*, a French song-story from the 12th century, which was staged in November 1924, with E. Carrick playing Aucassin and Gwen Sibley playing Nicolette. Gwen was one of the finest teachers of speech and drama in the City. The production was a resounding success, and made an excellent stepping-stone for future productions, proving that experimental and lesser-known classical plays could be given an airing and at the same time help to give a balanced programme throughout the year at the Little Theatre.

This was followed by a brilliant modern play which was to receive its first stage production in Hull, *The Charity that Began at Home*. Among its cast were names which many Hull people will remember today: Jenny Young, Ida Clark, Constance Clark, Charles Thompson, William Blakeney, Carrick Foster, Edgar Appleton, Leonard Munroe Clark and Dorothy Nichol (Thompson).

The Little Theatre continued with its local 'rep', becoming ever more popular. Hannchen Drasdo, a well-known figure in amateur drama circles, worked extremely hard as honorary general secretary to the theatre, and members of amateur companies carried out front-of-the-house duties in full evening dress, bringing elegance and friendliness to the evening's entertainment. Arthur Whatmore remarked at a reception in 1923 that no-one had done more for the repertory movement in Hull than had the president of the Hull Playgoers' Society: 'When I came to Hull 18 months ago, the first person to whom I was introduced was Tom Sheppard, who at once offered to assist the movement, and since then his untiring efforts have unquestionably placed the Little Theatre in the successful position it holds today,' he said.

As still happens, 'suggestive' advertising helped to fill a theatre. In March 1926, the *Eastern Morning News* reported: 'While on the subject of the Hull Playgoers' Society, a great controversy seems to have been brought about by the announcement that Elmer Rice's *The Adding Machine* is to be produced by Mrs James Downs at the Little Theatre. The majority of members appear to be scandalised at the sordid character of the plot and the outspoken details of the dialogue. If some of the indignant communications received by the president were to be published, there would not be a single seat available by the time of the first night of the production.' This turned out to be true!

Many of the literary-minded citizens of Hull were delighted that the Shakespeare Society had not buried Shakespeare's works as shadows of the past when they changed their name, but realised that they could not do without the Immortal Bard, so, close on the heels of the 'daring' play, came a production of *Romeo and Juliet*, directed by Haworth Earle. Some older theatre-lovers of the City may recall that Lawrence Nicholson played Romeo and Audrey Dannett played Juliet, and that they became engaged at that time and subsequently married and remained active members of Hull Playgoers for many years. Imagination and artistry were always to the fore in these productions, and Earle believed that it was possible to emphasise the emotion in a play by light and colour alone, without the usual trappings of the stage, so he experimented with this play-of-plays, in which it has been said Shakespeare breathed his deepest and richest notes of love. It was a successful venture, loved by the audience, who appeared to be part of the crowd at Verona as the players moved through the auditorium.

Craftsmanship
Hull Playgoers continued to fill in the gaps between seasons at the Little Theatre, and always provided plays of interest. *The Cinder Age*, by Norman Anglin, which dealt with life millions of years hence, when the crust of the earth had cooled and the sun had burnt out, was no exception. The costumes designed by Louise Jacobs, which were undeniably beautiful, set one wondering, by their mixture of the ancient, medieval and modern, whether, after all, life is destined to run in cycles. The scenic effects by Charles Thompson were masterly, and called forth repeated applause. The frozen earth and sun discovered by the intrepid explorers gave him an opportunity for a fine piece of craftsmanship in design and lighting.

The Little Theatre's professional company became more and more popular, and Hull audiences enjoyed seeing their favourite actors playing a variety of roles throughout the season. Names which spring to mind include Michael MacCowan, André Van Geyesingham, Frederick Piper, Colin Clive, Carl Bernard and Charles Lefaux. Interesting productions included *You Never Can Tell*, *Candida*, and *The Skin Game*.

In 1929, Hull Playgoers' Council decided that, with their membership rising to around 400, they were in need of alternative accommodation for their readings and a theatre which would provide them with facilities for staging experimental productions. After many meetings and discussions, and promises of financial help from members, it was decided to start the search. The Old Gaiety Picture House in the Market Place was available on a five-year lease, and it was decided to take up the offer. The building was splendidly equipped, and no great sum of money was needed for improvements. The deal was clinched in November, and after members, headed by Charles Thompson, had worked at high pressure night and day, the Society's New Playhouse opened on 6 December with a performance of three original one-act plays. Arthur Whatmore attended and wished the Society every success. The Hull Playgoers' Council were delighted with this co-operation, because they had always thought of the Little Theatre as their 'baby', and wished to continue their support of the repertory movement. Indeed, their members continued to play in many 'rep' productions.

In March 1930, Hull Playgoers' Society made history by giving the world's first modern-dress production of *Much Ado About Nothing* at the New Playhouse. It certainly created interest with its cocktails, foxtrots, plus-fours and typewriters. But, in the words of their president, 'This is not a stage joke but a serious attempt to bring new life and vividness to the play by stripping it of the convention of Elizabethan costumes and antiquated styles of acting'. The play was produced by F. R. Bell, who taught English at Hull Grammar School.

A few days later, towards the end of March, tragedy struck the Little Theatre. Fire broke out in the early hours of the morning, and it was estimated that £3,000–£4,000 worth of damage was done. Hull Playgoers' Society immediately offered their premises to the repertory company for as long as was needed. Arthur Whatmore was most grateful for the gesture, but, realising that the theatre held only about 400 people, he knew that it would not be a viable proposition. So, with much regret, the repertory company was disbanded and the Little Theatre was closed until refurbishments were completed.

It was also in 1930 that a blow fell upon the amateur theatre with the formation of Equity, which made it very difficult for professional companies to introduce local talent into their productions, even on a no-payment basis. This was obviously a good move to protect the professional actors, but one cannot help feeling that support for the commercial theatre suffered for a time in the provinces, as more and more amateur groups came into being.

Maintaining their reputation for the unusual, the Playgoers produced, for the first time in Hull, Karel Capek's robot play, *R.U.R.* Membership of the Society had now grown to 500, so competition for parts was very keen. Among those chosen were William Blakeney, Liege Kirkby, Douglas Stenhouse-Stewart (a Hull eye-specialist), and Leonard Munroe Clark. The report in the newspaper summed up its success: 'The Hull Playgoers, with the splendid audacity of Mrs James Downs, produced *R.U.R.*, a play that one would not expect to be exactly popular in the usual acceptance of the word. The night I was there the place was crowded out and an excellent performance it was. At the Galsworthy play the evening after at the repertory theatre there was a fairly good audience. Of course, one remembers that *R.U.R.* is unique, and that Galsworthy is – well, Galsworthy . . .'

In December 1930, *A Winter's Tale* was produced by Haworth Earle. There was a delightful blend of tragedy and comedy, with a fragrant picture of rural merriment serving as a foil to the strong drama of jealousy and injured innocence. Phyllis Sharrah, whose mother, Madame Sharrah, owned one of the largest dancing academies in the town, arranged all the pastoral dances and ballets, which brought colour and lightness to the production.

Keeping up their traditions of presenting unusual plays, in 1931 they put on a production of Carlo Goldoni's *Daughters are Dutiful*. It was translated by two members of the Society, C. H. Hocking and Charles Thompson, the scenic director, and the production was the first to be performed on the English stage. Comedy was to the fore in this season, which included Shaw's *Man and Superman* and a production of *Twelfth Night* specially for children. Constance Clarke made of it 'a Shakespeare pantomime which was rollicking and as light as air.' The Education Committee thanked the Playgoers' Society for the arrangements they had made for free attendance of school children at one of their performances.

Persistence pays

In 1932, the British Drama League held a conference in Hull, and the Playgoers put on a production for the delegates of *The Yellow Jacket*, by George Hazleton and G. H. Bearimo, a comedy in the Chinese manner. It was the most costly show that had been mounted up to then. Except for a West End production some years previously, the play had not been performed, and L. and R. Nathan Limited, who were associated with the London production, dressed the show throughout.

There were no lengths to which the Playgoers would not go to find exactly what was necessary to make a play authentic. In this production, Chinese music by Low Chung, Chinatown, Liverpool, was needed, and the real Chinese gramophone records were required. The search started at the headquarters of the principal gramophone firms; a catalogue was available, but it was said that there were no records in England. Through the editor of The Gramophone, they even reached the Chinese Legation – but no joy. Who would have thought that a Chinese laundry would be the answer to a society's prayer? It was here that they found the address of Low Chung, and the director, Mrs James Downs, tracked him down to a Chinese grocery store in a curious little street in the dockside quarter of Liverpool. She emerged from the shop with a parcel of records under her arm – and other genuine Chinese properties.

It is often said in the amateur movement that the classics do not draw an audience, but Hull Playgoers have proved this wrong many times. In 1931 they produced Shaw's *Fanny's First Play*, a play that loses not one jot of its high spirits by touching philosophic heights and depths. This was so successful that four repeat performances had to be sandwiched into a busy programme. It was noted in a current local newspaper that the prowess of local theatrical enterprises had long been recognised as a strong force for putting Hull on the map. This was emphasised in a novel fashion by a Blackburn man who, when he retired from business, set up house in Hull chiefly on account of the strong theatrical movement in the city. In fact, he was one of a number of residents from other towns who figured in the Hull Playgoers' mailing list, and who made special journeys to Hull for each production at the New Playhouse.

Another memorable production was *The Wild Duck*. This was the first time the Society had tackled an Ibsen play. Satirists and jokers at the time had a habit of poking fun at Ibsen and his Continental disciples on the grounds of their supposed gloom and morbidity. Critics spoke of him as 'a tomb, a violent and shattering explosion in the theatre of today'. Only George Bernard Shaw praised his insight and his genius as a story-teller. However, one member of the audience leaving the New Playhouse after a performance of *The Wild Duck* was heard to say that he had been 'filled with that pity and terror which, according to Aristotle, is always the outcome of great tragedy'.

It is imperative for the theatre to attract an audience. Hull Playgoers were never short of publicity gimmicks. When they chose a crime play in which the solution was left to the audience, they invited the chiefs of the local C.I.D. and leading figures in the legal profession to the performance. The play was *Somebody Knows*, by John Van Druten, who set down in his dialogue all the facts about a murder and subsequent trial except the central one. Whether or not the audience solved the mystery has not been handed down to posterity – but the Society played to full houses. Variety cannot be said to have been absent from the Playgoers' programme, for their production of *The Knight of the Burning Pestle*, by Beaumont and Fletcher, provoked loud laughs rather than intellectual smiles. They romped home with a cast suitably equipped for the task, including Ronald Dufton, Clive Dugdale, Nancy Wheelhouse, Ida Clark and many others.

Expansion

Meanwhile, the Little Theatre continued to prosper, mounting plays for one week in the early days, and eventually playing for two weeks. Many names spring to mind of actors and actresses who have since become well-known in the theatrical world – Margaretta Scott, James Stewart Granger, Ronald Culver, Edith Sharpe, William Mervyn, Martin Bradley, Carl Bernard, Ambrosine Phillpotts, Jack Minster and many more. Mervyn and Bradley both started their careers as members of Hull Playgoers

In 1933, the newly-appointed manager of the Little Theatre, Peppino Santangelo, was beginning to think about expansion, and was looking for a theatre capable of presenting the best of all types of entertainment.

Eventually, the old Assembly Rooms became vacant, and, although Hull Fire Brigade had hoped to extend their premises in that direction, they gave way, and the building was taken over by Santangelo in 1937. A tremendous amount of constructional work was needed before it was converted into a theatre, and building was still in progress when war broke out in 1939, but Santangelo never gave up hope, and he persuaded the directors to keep up the work until it was complete. Many theatres, of course, closed on the outbreak of war.

It had been the intention to open the New Theatre with a season of repertory, including appearances by Tom Walls, a great attraction in those days, but call-ups made it impossible to be sure of keeping a company together, so it was decided to turn to touring companies. In October 1939, the New Theatre opened with *Me and My Girl*, and this was followed by the Vic Wells Ballet. Then Santangelo was again fortunate (after much haggling with the powers-that-be in London to prove that Hull could be a viable proposition for cultural productions) in being able to mount a production by the Vic Wells Opera Company at the theatre. However, financial difficulties struck again, and it was back to a repertory company for a time. In the early 1940s, however, there was heavy bombing in London, and it is an ill wind that blows nobody any good, for Peppino Santangelo realised that West End productions were now looking for venues in the provinces, and with his perfect sense of timing, he jumped in and ensured that Hull enjoyed many lavish productions of opera, ballet, musicals and straight plays.

Closure, re-birth

To return to the Playgoers: in 1940 the secretary, Liege Kirkby, was called up and could no longer fulfil his commitments, so an informal meeting was called and it was decided to close down for the duration, though many members did invaluable work in the entertainment field with E.N.S.A. When the war ended in 1945, a public meeting was called to find out what response there would be to the re-opening of the Society. Enthusiasm was still evident, so the fortnightly readings were re-introduced and the Society began to live once more, enjoying *Lady Windermere's Fan, Man and Superman, Juno and the Paycock* and many other fine plays.

The first production after the war was in 1945, a one-act play for the British Drama League competition. I was asked to produce Act 3 from Shaw's *Major Barbara*, and it was a great success in the first round, held in the College of Commerce Lecture Theatre. The company, thinking that they were ready for stardom, journeyed to Scunthorpe for the second round, only to be slated by the adjudicator for choosing an extract from a three-act play. You soon learn in the theatre that in order to have triumphs you must suffer many knocks!

The next production was, however, considered to be one of the triumphs. This was also put on at the College of Commerce Theatre, and was T. S. Eliot's *The Family Reunion*, directed by an American, Betty Dickenson, who was living in Hull for a short time. Leading roles were played by Kenneth Hibbert, Dorothy Thompson, Hilda Atkins, Elyse Harrison, Liege Kirkby and myself. This played to capacity houses, and it is interesting to recall that the royalties were £4. 4s for the first performance and £3. 3s. for subsequent ones, and that the show made a profit of £12. 15s. 4d., which was felt to be 'very satisfactory'!

By 1949, it was obvious that societies were having difficulties in encouraging young men into the acting world. C. S. Thompson, an active member of the Society, proposed that it should offer free scholarships in speech training to up to half-a-dozen boys of secondary school age, who should be made honorary members during the training period. The scheme did not appear to get off the ground, but the Society did not give up its efforts to encourage young members, and in 1951 it was proposed that a Junior Section should be established. As a result, the Playgoers' Workshop was formed. I was its first chairman and Beryl Ashburn was secretary. The first production, *The Giaconda Smile*, by Aldous Huxley, was performed at St Stephen's Church Hall, now the Spring Street Theatre. Although the production was a great success, with Margaret Broadley playing the lead, the Workshop suffered a loss of £7. 14s. 11d.

Several productions followed, including *Joy*, by John Galsworthy, in which one member of the cast was Michael Barton, a member of the family which helped found the Cottingham Drama Society. He went on to occupy a very good position with the B.B.C. However, in 1953, after more financial losses, it was decided to dissolve the Workshop.

The Society continued its fortnightly readings in the Church Institute in Albion Street, and on the closure of the Institute it moved to the Methodist Church Hall in Prospect Street and then to the Young People's Institute in George Street, where it is still meeting today. One production was mounted each year, and the venues varied according to availability and economy. They included University College Assembly Hall, Hymers College Memorial Hall, the Farmery Hall in George Street, St Mary's Grammar School and the Library Theatre.

On the Society's 50th anniversary in 1951, there was a notable production of Jean Anouilh's *Ring Round the Moon*, which was directed by Ronald Dufton. This was played in the Memorial Hall of Hymers College by courtesy of the headmaster, Harry Roach. I am sure that those who saw this production cannot fail to remember the 'note-tearing' scene between Isabella (Jennifer Ainley) and Mr Messerschmann (Harry Roach), which never failed to produce an ovation. The ballroom scene was designed and built by Clifford Ashburn and Denis Ringham, and was a joy to see, with fairy lights and lanterns transforming the stage into a ballroom and

8

conservatory. In spite of the fact that a tin of white paint was tipped over most of the stage and decor – and, indeed, the piano – on the evening before the opening, everything looked spick and span on the night!

The Society, like all others, suffered many setbacks, mostly financial. This included the loss of costumes and properties which had been stored in disused Northern Dairies premises. The precious bits and pieces had moved around from pillar to post for some years, and eventually, by a 'gentlemen's agreement' – alas, no written word – they were collected and taken to this apparently heaven-sent home. Unfortunately, in 1969 a third party took over the building and, unbeknown to the Society, it was demolished along with all the 'treasures'.

In 1969, Hull Playgoers welcomed Tom Martin, a lecturer at Hull College of Education, as president. Not only did he make a fine president and an excellent director, but he also provided the Society with many young members, both in the acting and the stage-management field, several of whom are still members today. During the years between 1969 and 1980, some extremely fine productions were put on at the Library Theatre, including *A Man for All Seasons, Caesar and Cleopatra*, and *The Importance of Being Earnest*.

Royal pageant
Perhaps one of the most memorable performances of this period was *This Royal Throne*, mounted to celebrate the Queen's Silver Jubilee in 1977. This was a royal pageant through the ages, colourful, moving and at times amusing. The show was devised by Tom Martin and Pamela Coates, and comprised a selection of extracts from ten different plays by some of the world's greatest writers, Shaw and Shakespeare among them. The episodes were linked by commentary spoken by players portraying Charles Dickens and Jane Austen, and those taking part included Gregan Davis as Henry II and Geoffrey Annis as Beckett; John Andrew as Henry V; Honor Pallant as Mary, Queen of Scots; Kay Stevens as Elizabeth I; and Lorna Kirkby as the Queen Mother.

In 1980, the Society used the Spring Street Theatre for the first time, with a lively production of Dylan Thomas's *Under Milk Wood*. Honor Pallant directed this with great skill, introducing many children into the large cast, and the set was a feat in itself. On stage were a boat, a double bed, and all the village houses, including Captain Cat's lookout window – and there was still room to perform and dance. The show played to capacity houses – some would-be patrons had to be turned away – and it was a financial as well as an artistic success.

It is impossible to do justice to all the fine performances and productions which have taken place over the years. Hull Playgoers have been fortunate in having had the opportunity to play in the Spring Street

Theatre, and it is true to say that their choice of plays has been demanding, interesting and in line with the tradition of presenting the best in modern and classical drama. They are fortunate in having members who enjoy directing, and who have had considerable experience in this field, including Gregan Davis, Vera Gorringe and myself. Plays presented over the past two or three years have included *A Chorus of Disapproval*, by Alan Ayckbourn, *The Daughter-in-Law*, by D.H. Lawrence, and *Antigone*, by Jean Anouilh – quite a range. Hull Playgoers' Society celebrated their 90th anniversary in 1991-92, going back to their beginnings and producing a selection of Shakespearean works, proving that they had not forgotten their roots, the Shakespeare Society, which emerged in 1901 and has continued to live and to overcome many difficulties.

The New Theatre has had its ups and downs too, but is still doing a fine job in the 1990s. On 5 March 1951, it was purchased by the Whitehall Theatre Ltd for £78,000, Peppino Santangelo being retained as General Administrator. Coincidentally, of course, it was in the London Whitehall farces that the East Yorkshire comedy actor Brian (now Sir Brian) Rix made his name, but on the administrative side the local link was George Jager, MP for Goole, who was the theatre company's secretary. In February 1958, the company put the New Theatre up for sale, and it was announced that Mr Santangelo was to retire in the April. For three years the fate of the theatre hung in the balance. The Whitehall Company continued to operate it, but a syndicate ran bingo sessions on Sundays and eventually offered to take over the building. There was also a suggestion that the theatre should be converted into flats, which were then much sought-after in the city centre.

However, a campaign, in which the Playgoers' Society played no small part, was mounted to save the theatre. On 3 February 1958, the *Hull Daily Mail* reported, 'A petition under the banner, "Make the New Theatre your own" was launched in Hull on Saturday night. Nearly 500 signatures were collected at the theatre and at a performance by Hull Playgoers' Society.' Finally, on 28 September 1961, the newspaper was able to announce, 'Hull to buy the New Theatre'; the Corporation purchased it for £50,000 and proceeded to run it as a limited company under a 21-member Council of Management. So, may both amateur and professional theatres continue into the 21st century and beyond!

Well-known actors and actresses at the Little Theatre
James Stewart Granger, Michael MacCowan, Frederick Piper, Leslie Kyle, André Van Geycsingham, Charles Lefaux, Cail Bernard, James Mason, Maurice Denham, Roland Culver, William Mervyn, Margaretta Scott, Enid Hewitt, Ambrosine Phillpotts, Edith Sharpe, Helen Shingler.

Major productions at Hull Repertory Theatre

The Romantic Age	A. A. Milne
John Gabriel Borkman	H. Ibsen
The Ship	St John Ervine
The Circle	W. Somerset Maugham
You Never Can Tell	G. B. Shaw
The Liar	Goldoni
Sweeny Todd	F. Hazleton
The Cradle Song	G. Martinez
Granite	Clemence Dane
Arms and the Man	G. B. Shaw
She Stoops to Conquer	Oliver Goldsmith
The First Mrs Fraser	St John Ervine
Richard of Bordeaux	Gordon Daviot

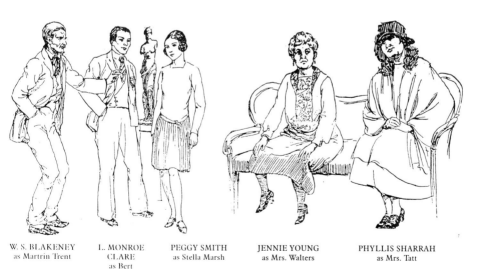

W. S. BLAKENEY
as Martrin Trent

L. MONROE
CLARE
as Bert

PEGGY SMITH
as Stella Marsh

JENNIE YOUNG
as Mrs. Walters

PHYLLIS SHARRAH
as Mrs. Tatt

Scenes from Bert's Girls *at the Little Theatre, December, 1927.*

The Yellow Jacket, *by George Hazleton and G. H. Bearimo, 1932. The music and props for this show were eventually found in a Chinese grocery store in Liverpool's docklands*

The Family Reunion, *1948. In the picture are Kenneth Hibbert, Teddy Tilley, Liege Kirkby, Dorothy Thompson, Margaret Burnett, June Robinson, Elyse Stothard and Bill Blakeney.*

Hannchen Drasco

Kay Stevens as Queen Eleanor in Tom Martin's production of Anouth's Beckett, *1964.*

The photograph was taken outside Beverley Minster during the
St John of Beverley Festival.

The Assembly Rooms in Kingston Square, Hull, in April, 1939, as demolition proceeded to create the New Theatre. The photograph, taken by Hannchen Drasdo, is by courtesy of Lee Drasdo.

13

TWO THEATRES OF THE THIRTIES AND FORTIES

THE HOUSE OF SHARRAH

By Sadie Ellerby

TWO REMARKABLE WOMEN, Alice Sharrah and her daughter, Phyllis, made an impact on the music and drama scene in Hull which was to span well over half a century.

Alice Sharrah founded the Hull School of Music at 22, Reed Street in 1886, after having had an all-round musical and theatrical training, and her first pupils studied piano, singing and elocution. After only one year, Alice presented her first recital, in the Royal Institution, with 20 pupils taking part. She engaged other teachers to assist her, and by 1888-89 her entertainments featured singing – solo and choral – sketches, percussion band, and items on piano, violin, guitar, mandoline and banjo.

In 1888, she became local secretary for the Trinity College of Music, London, a position she held for the rest of her life, and by 1891, dancing had been added to the curriculum of subjects taught at the school, which, in 1892, was moved from Reed Street into larger premises at 21, Story Street.

In September 1894, Alice married Henry Simpson, but she always retained the name of Sharrah for professional purposes, and from 1902 we find her referred to as 'Madame Alice Sharrah', the name under which she is remembered.

Phyllis was born in 1895, and by the time her brother, Guy, was born in 1899, Alice and her husband had moved into the large house at 55, Spring Bank, which from then on was the headquarters of the school. According to Press cuttings, Phyllis was something of an infant prodigy, giving dramatic recitals, including Shakespearean speeches, at the age of seven, and by the age of eight she had already passed two piano examinations. In addition to her studies at her mother's school, Phyllis attended boarding school – St Mary's Convent in York – and also studied on the Continent, latterly at the Conservatoire in Lindau, Germany.

October 1906 saw the publication of the first issue of 'HSM', the school's quarterly magazine. Illustrations include photographs of the 'Reception Room', the drawing-room of 55, Spring Bank, where Alice interviewed prospective students and their parents. In later years, Alice used this as her studio, where her private students had their lessons.

Other photographs feature the school proper: this was a two-storey building erected at the bottom of the garden, fronting on to Grey Street, so that it was not necessary to go through the house to get to the school. This was the building which I knew as a pupil of the school, and as a member of the Sharrah Drama Club.

The ground floor consisted of a long room, the floor covered with linoleum, and this was where we had our tap classes. It was also used as a rehearsal room. Along one side were a number of small practice-rooms with pianos, and at the end of the long room, overlooking the garden, was a small, square studio, also with a piano, for private drama and singing lessons. Later, when Phyllis was in charge of the school, this became her studio. On the opposite side of this room was a staircase leading up to the Music Room, which had a small stage at one end. Here Madame held her school prize-givings and small concerts. It was our ballet studio, and also served as a rehearsal room.

In the years up to the First World War, Madame Sharrah's entertainments became ever more ambitious. By 1909, she had a school orchestra, a male-voice choir and a French elocution class, in addition to all her other classes. There were regular performances in French, and concert performances of grand operas. The variety entertainments featured excerpts from opera, musical comedy, ballet and Shakespeare! The venues she used were the Assembly Rooms, the Royal Institution and the Grand Theatre. She even devised and staged a number of historical pageants. Open-air performances of Shakespeare's plays in the grounds of Tranby Croft, then the home of the Wilson family, were another regular feature.

At a Press interview in 1909, Alice recalled that, when she started her school, the only amateur performing society was the East Yorkshire Dramatic Society. Many of her pupils became leading members of the societies which came into being around the turn of the century – the Hull Shakespeare Society, the Hull Amateur Operatic Society and the Hull Dramatic Society among them.

Alice Sharrah died in 1940.

Handed On

Her educational and theatrical training completed, Phyllis spent some years in the professional theatre, including London's West End, before returning to Hull to assist her mother in running the school.

As a performer, Phyllis had appeared regularly with the Hull Shakespeare Society before the First World War, and on her return to the City she played with the Hull Playgoers' Society, as did many of her pupils. When she took control of the school, there was much greater emphasis on verse-speaking, dramatic art and dance. Musical tuition continued, though to a lesser extent than before, under Miss Lily Marshall. Many Hull School of Music students appeared with the Hull Repertory Company from its formation in 1924 until it ceased in 1939. Some pupils became student members of the company, among them Joan Riley, who was Assistant Stage Manager in the 1930s. Joan, the widow of Frederick Piper (who in his early years was a member of the Hull company), still directs at Windsor's Theatre Royal and is a member of the Board.

For a number of years in the mid-1930s, the Denville Repertory Company were in residence at Hull's Alexandra Theatre, and often called on the Hull School of Music to augment their casts. There was a dearth of opera in Hull between the wars, particularly after the conversion of the Grand Theatre into a cinema in 1928, but companies such as the Carl Rosa and Moody Manners also called on the Hull School of Music to enhance their chorus-line. Like her mother, Phyllis believed in presenting her pupils to the public. The spectacular entertainments she devised were presented at the Alexandra and Palace Theatres, and in these Phyllis excelled both as director and as choreographer.

In the 1920s and 30s, cabaret became increasingly popular, particularly as interval entertainment at balls and dances and during dinner in hotels and restaurants. Almost every week during the winter months, Phyllis sent out teams of dancers and entertainers to such functions, drawn from among the school's pupils and, later, members of the Sharrah Drama Club.

Another field on which Phyllis concentrated before the Second World War was pantomime, recruiting and training teams of 'Babes' for these popular seasonal shows, not only in Hull but as far away as Sheffield. My own first appearance in a professional theatre was as a 'Babe'; that career was short-lived, however, for by the following year I had grown too tall!

Up to the 1930s, many pupils had been able to study at the school full-time, but from then on most had to work for a living and could study only part-time.

The Drama Club

In June 1934, the verse-speaking and dramatic art students of the Hull School of Music held a meeting to form a social and dramatic club, with the school as its headquarters. A constitution was drawn up and the club came into being in October the same year.. The members at that time numbered 16 and the producer, of course, was Phyllis Sharrah. By 1938, the club was performing under the name of 'The Drama Club', and in that year a junior section was formed, 'Hull Junior Drama Club'. Initially, membership of the clubs was confined to students of the school, but by 1939 this rule had been relaxed so far as the senior club was concerned From then until its closure in 1958, the club was, in Phyllis's words, 'exclusively for people who are really keen on the theatre'. Entrance was always by ballot only

16

The club's first full-length production was of Clemence Dane's *Will Shakespeare*, with Arthur Burrell and Marie Wing playing the leading roles of Shakespeare and Queen Elizabeth I, shortly before they both 'turned professional'. This was in October 1937, and a month later the club took part in a full-length play competition run by the *News Chronicle* newspaper. An unusual aspect of this competition was that all the groups had to perform the same play – *Mystery at Greenfingers*, which had been specially written for the competition by J. B. Priestley.

The aim of the club was to present at least two full-length plays each year and to participate in both full-length and one-act play competitions. The only suitable venue in the City centre for amateur productions was the Royal Institution, which was destroyed in the 1941 blitz. Throughout the life of the club, however, Phyllis was always willing to take productions on tour if alternative venues became available, or if she was invited to do so and, like her mother before her, she was always willing to present any of the school or club entertainments for the benefit of charities. A special feature of the club was that Thursday nights were set aside as 'Club Nights', those present signing the club book. On the first Thursday in the month an entertainment was presented in the upstairs Music Room, each one being the responsibility of a different club member.

The 1938 productions were the American comedy, *Nothing but the Truth*, put on in the April, and Emlyn Williams's *Night Must Fall* in the November. February 1939 saw the presentation of Christa Winslowe's *Children in Uniform* as an entry in the British Drama League's full-length play competition. The Garrett Players presented *Berkeley Square*, and the Malet Lambert Old Students Drama Circle *Tobias and the Angel*, both of which appeared in the final held in Buxton. The Sharrah Club was not so fortunate, but Stanley Williscroft, who stage-managed *Children in Uniform*, played one of the leads in *Berkeley Square*, and I had a small part in both the club and the Malet Lambert plays.

The spring of 1939 saw both the senior and the junior clubs competing in one-act festivals and a large number of pupils of all ages competing in musical festivals, both in verse-speaking and drama and in the various dancing classes. A full-length production of J. M. Barrie's *Dear Brutus* was planned for the autumn.

In February 1940, the club presented another full-length play, *Nine Till Six*, by Aimee and Philip Stuart, in the Royal Institution and took it on tour to the Spa Theatre, Bridlington. In both places, performances were in aid of War Charities. The Bridlington set had been put together for us by the Spa Theatre staff. I disobeyed instructions and did not 'walk the set' before the show, so I was not aware that the door opened the opposite way from the one we had used in Hull. I had an exit line which went something like 'See you in the morning if nothing's happened to me!' I tried to open the door, but because I was pulling instead of pushing, it jammed. I could hear Phyllis cursing and struggling with the door on the other side, all to no avail. Meantime, the audience were roaring with laughter. Eventually, I managed to squeeze between the edge of the door-flat and the tormentor. What Phyllis said to me is unprintable, but it taught me a lesson which I have never forgotten!

In April 1940, the club presented its last plays until after the war. The performance was entitled, *Comedy Cocktail* and consisted of two one-act plays, *Two Gentlemen of Soho*, by A. P. Herbert, with Phyllis herself in the leading role of the Duchess of Canterbury, and *The Magic Suit*, by M. Moiseiwitsch, the first stage play featuring the radio character 'Mr Penny'. These were followed by one hour of concert party entertainment.

Throughout the war, the Thursday Club Nights were maintained. However, the monthly First Thursday entertainments were moved to the first Saturday afternoons in the month from 5 October 1940. These entertainments gave us the opportunity of trying out new numbers for our Charades shows.

Post-war Plays.
The role played by the Sharrah Drama Club and its offshoot concert party, The Charades, during the war, has been outlined in my article on the Voluntary Entertainment Service. The first full-length play to be put on after hostilities ceased was *The First Mrs Fraser*, by St John Ervine, which went on stage on 13 September 1945, a week after Victory in Japan Day. *Winter Sunshine* followed in December 1945, and Priestley's *They Came to a City* in February 1946. I had been called up in the summer of 1944 and returned on 4 January 1946, in time to help build the Priestley play set. Of these productions, the most suitable to tour was *The First Mrs Fraser*, and I remember our taking it to Thirsk and Snaith, both of which had been outside our area during the war.

The following year was a very active one for the club, with three more new productions. Our regular pre-war venue, the Royal Institution, having been bombed, we had to find a new home; the choice fell on the old Assembly Hall of the University College, now Hull University. As an experiment, the second production of 1946, Ivor Novello's *Fresh Fields*, was presented at the Co-op Hall in Kingston Square, but this did not prove to be very satisfactory, so we returned to the Assembly Hall in September with another St John Ervine play, *Robert's Wife*, and in the November with the Quinteros' play, *A Hundred Years Old*, both plays being toured.

I particularly remember how effective our set looked on the larger stage of the Spa Theatre in Bridlington. Remembering the set problem of our previous visit, we started touring our own, and, for venues unable to accommodate our scenery, we had alternative settings using curtains, some of which had started life on the stage of the school's Music Room! At the Assembly Hall in 1947, we played *East Lynne* in the January and a new production of *Nothing but the Truth* in the September. In the spring of that year, most of the club members had been involved in Phyllis's production of *1066 And All That* at the New Theatre, which had marked the end of the VES organisation – and my debut as Stage Manager at the New. In 1948 there were productions in January of Drinkwater's *A Man's House*, and in September of C. L. Anthony's *Touch Wood*, again at the University College, and once more we toured. By this time, a regular port of call for our productions was the Village Hall at North Cave.

The following year saw Phyllis's first post-war Shakespeare production, *The Merchant of Venice*, at the Assembly Hall in the January, repeated in July in the Open Air Theatre in Pearson Park. Meantime, the Club Nights and First Thursday entertainments continued to be held.

On Saturday, 5 March 1949, a nostalgic event took place in the Reception Room of the Hull Guildhall – the 'stand down' performance of the Charades Concert Party, the programme including some of the original numbers and featuring some of the members of the concert party who had returned from war service. It was more than a final show; it was put on to help raise funds for the Arthur Burrell Memorial Trophy. Arthur, one of Phyllis's pupils, had been one of the leading actors in Hull, playing not only with the club but with the Hull Repertory Company before continuing his professional career with the Sheldon-Browne Company. A warm, generous actor, he would obviously have had a great future in the theatre, but he unhesitatingly abandoned his career to enlist in the Royal Air Force, reaching the rank of Flight Lieutenant before being killed in action over Sicily.

When Phyllis first suggested the idea of a trophy in his memory, to be awarded for acting excellence in festival competitions, there was overwhelming support, not only from members of the school and the club but from his many admirers. The magnificent silver trophy which was eventually purchased represented Arthur as Will Shakespeare, the role he had played in the Sharrah Drama Club's first production. It has been used by both the British Drama League and the Hull Musical Festival, and at present it is the award for the Festival's Open Shakespeare Character Study class, recent winners including Jody Crozier, of the Northern Theatre Company School (1989) and Catherine Harvey, granddaughter of Stella Sizer-Simpson (1990).

The Final Curtain

The school continued, but Phyllis restricted her drama teaching to private pupils, whom she regularly entered for festivals and examinations. Dancing tuition also continued, Phyllis entering teams of dancers in festivals, and providing dancers and choreography for local operatic society productions. She was also actively involved with the New Theatre's Sunday Theatre Club and the Hull and District Theatre Guild, and was a member of the committees of both the Hull Musical Festival and the local branch of the British Drama League.

Meantime, the club tried out different venues for its full-length productions. Eliot's *The Cocktail Party* was put on in St Stephen's Hall, Spring Street, now the Spring Street Theatre; my production of *Dangerous Corner*, by J. B. Priestley, was staged in the large hall of the YPI; and with Maugham's *The Sacred Flame* we were back in the Assembly Hall, the same hall being used for *Begone, Dull Care*, written in the 1950s by David Kelsey, a past pupil turned professional.

The club returned to the Open Air Theatre with a production of *The Tempest*, and presented Galsworthy's *The Show* in Stella Sizer-Simpson's Janus Theatre on Hessle Road, while *Arsenic and Old Lace* was put on in the parish hall of All Saints' Church, Margaret Street.

Towards the end of her time in Hull, Phyllis had to sell the school premises fronting on to Grey Street, the building becoming the Rediffusion Social Club. The Sharrah Club rented a couple of stables on the other side of Grey Street as a scenery store, but there was very little room inside in which to work, so most of the set-building had to be done in the open air. I recall working in the snow on the set for *East Lynne*, with Hilary Boynton, of the College of Education, who had been engaged by Phyllis as scenic artist (I think she thought the Victorian decor she wanted was beyond me!). The loss of the school premises meant that the big Reception Room on the ground floor of 55 Spring Bank became the rehearsal room and dance studio, and the large front bedroom a second studio. Furniture, props and costumes had to be stored on the upper floors.

Phyllis Sharrah left Hull in 1958: it was the end of an era . . .

Footnote: Many members of the Sharrah Drama Club have been – or still are – well known in local drama circles. They include May Donnison and Audrey and Herbert Baker (Hull Amateur Operatic Society), Robert Morton and his wife, Nora Hagland, Paddy Shephard and Denis Ringham (all Hull Playgoers), Peter Lund (Beverley Operatic Society), Bertram Wood (Hull Playgoers and Hessle Amateur Operatic and Dramatic Society), Betty Carver (Mrs Teddy Lorrimar, singing teacher and member of Hull Opera Centre), Maureen Leathley (ballet mistress for the Carl Rosa Opera Company and dancing teacher) and Jack and Dorothy Cawthorne (Hull Garret Players). I also had varying spells with all four operatic societies, Hull Opera Centre, Malet Lambert Old Students Drama Club and the Playgoers' Workshop, besides stints of professional stage management.

THE DRASDO 'REP'

By Gillian Holtby

With acknowledgements to Paul Drasdo, Lee Drasdo, Geoffrey Bayldon, Billie Lee and Elinor Stark

TURN THE PAGES of the *Hull Daily Mail* for any season of any year from 1908, when she made her debut, to her obituary notices in 1963, and whenever drama in the area is the subject, the name of Hannchen Margaretta Drasdo is almost certainly involved. An elocutionist and performer of distinction, a revered teacher, and an amateur producer of rare quality, she commanded a following throughout her life. When, as a girl, she appeared as the 'principal artiste' in a recital at the Lecture Hall in 1908, the newspaper enthused: 'Above medium height, with most expressive eyes, pretty fair hair, svelte figure and fine carriage, she possesses a well-toned voice and a fund of vitality which gives life and reality to the ideas and sentiments expressed.'

It was her father who gave her the nickname by which she was so affectionately known, 'Hannchen' being a diminutive for Johanna, her baptismal name. Paul Julius Drasdo was a striking figure in Hull in the late 19th century. He was the principal immigration agent for the Jewish refugees fleeing from the pogroms in Russia by the crossing from Hamburg to Hull, from where they moved on to Liverpool and the United States, though a number settled here, and others in the Leeds area. The business closed when America introduced immigration barriers.

Hannchen, like her father, spoke German, and her other talents had also been passed down. Her grandfather had been keenly interested in acting, and her father had a fine singing voice. From her early years at Ellerslie House School, she studied 'elocution', as voice-production for the theatre would then be termed, and went on to London in 1907 to continue her training with a view to professional performances. In that year, her first advertisement appeared: 'Miss Drasdo is open to accept Engagements for Concerts, Recitals, At Homes etc.' These performances developed considerably, embracing classical excerpts, monologues, humorous sketches and poetry of all kinds in an eclectic repertoire that gained her growing popularity, not only in her native city but also in Scandinavia. She made several tours abroad, and Norway, in particular, seems to have welcomed her warmly, the Press praising her exemplary spoken English and theatrical abilities – indeed, in one instance her two-week engagement was extended to three to meet the demand for tickets! And these tours were not confined to the concert platform, or the hosting literary societies; all along, she volunteered her services to any school that cared to approach her.

Hannchen was closely involved not only with the theatrical scene in Hull but also with the Hull Ladies Musical Union, with which she had a long association. It was at her instigation that the choir toured Norway in 1914, giving a number of concerts, one in the presence of the Queen of Norway.

A long-standing member of the Playgoers' Society – and on record as having created a formidable Lady Bracknell for the East Yorkshire Dramatic Society – she was well aware of the Little Theatre movement which was gathering momentum after the First World War and, indeed, she wrote on the topic in *Theatre World*. It was inevitable, therefore, that she should be at the centre of plans to establish the Hull Little Theatre in 1924. She served as organising secretary for the planning committee which was led by Tom Sheppard and James Downes to back Arthur Whatmore, the professional producer who offered to run the first repertory season in the old Kingston Square Lecture Hall premises adjoining the Assembly Rooms, and she worked indefatigably to promote this courageous venture in every possible way.

Her work included fund-raising, ticket-selling, publicity and leading a team of volunteers to staff the front-of-house. Such was her charisma that to be a member of this team conferred great social cachet. The local Press reviewed not only the play and stage costumes but what was worn by Miss Drasdo's team as well! She herself was typically reported as being 'smart in black, with touches of rose in the shoulder scarves.' Her zeal in helping the theatre to pay its way even extended to picking up and taking home discarded programmes so that she and her brother, Ralph, could clean them up and iron them for re-sale.

As organising secretary, and later director, of the Hull Repertory Company, she earned tributes for her dedication from all concerned, including the President, his committee, and a succession of theatre directors, actors and actresses. She did this on top of a busy life of teaching and recitals, and she claimed to be 'quite exasperated' with being for ever lauded in the minutes of annual general meetings and in Press coverage as 'energetic and capable'. Her repertory theatre involvement continued until the Second World War halted the creation of a larger and more sophisticated theatre in the rebuilt Assembly Rooms – the New Theatre. Miss Drasdo's own 'snaps' of this rebuilding illustrate just what an undertaking it was, and bear witness to the courage required to complete the work during the uncertainties of the early months of the war.

In the inter-war years, she found time to pursue another theatrical interest, marionettes. Together with Mrs Roper Spencer, she made string puppets herself, some as much as three feet tall, and, as the Drasdo Marionette Company, toured the puppet shows widely, one performance being in the Ellen Terry Memorial Theatre at Smallhythe, at the invitation of Edith Craig. Verbal history has it that some of these puppets found their way into the Hull Museum, which has, indeed, some marionettes, though without any identification, alas.

Keen driver
Hannchen Drasdo was the first woman in Hull to gain a driving licence, and as a young woman she was a familiar sight in her father's old Vauxhall open tourer. Later, with a close friend, Margaret Geddes, she toured Europe in a small, eccentric Austin known as 'Bill', a euphemism for the term used by an uncle who, on first seeing the car, exclaimed, 'What a b . . . !'

On the death of her father, she moved from the family home, 81, Beverley Road, Hull, where she had served so successfully as his hostess and housekeeper that, in 1901, the Humber Lodge of Freemasons presented her with a silver hand-mirror in recognition of her support to him during his year of office as Worshipful Master of the Lodge. Her new home was at 14, Westbourne Avenue, where, in a large, blue-carpeted front room crammed with books and possessing a sunny, comfortable window-seat, she taught her pupils from a big easy-chair. The outbreak of war caught her motoring in the South of France, and she drove the 897 miles to the Channel non-stop in 24 hours! War heralded the closure of all theatres, but gradually it was realised that public morale demanded entertainment, and shows re-opened at hours limited by the need to avoid travel in the blackout. The New Theatre initially had to forgo 'rep' for touring shows.

In September 1940, the *Hull Daily Mail* described the work with which Miss Drasdo had become involved, even to the extent of buying her own van in which to transport scenery and props: 'Entertainment for the troops, the job which started out as a great lark, has lost none of its joy, but has more and more taken on an aspect of national importance. For nearly a year, concert parties and plays have been going out to the loneliest, most isolated outposts, wherever men are stationed, to while away a few hours . . . Few nights pass without some little troupe going out somewhere, silently and without fuss, doing their job, their only reward the acclamation of the men they entertain.'

It was the Lord Mayor of the time, Alderman Hewitt, who first suggested to Hannchen Drasdo that she undertake an open air production as part of a civic programme entitled 'Stay at Home Holiday'. These programmes were intended to persuade people to forgo any wartime travel on the cut-back and congested railway system, on which troops had to take priority. Hannchen responded with her Drasdo Repertory Company. Initially, in 1942, she directed *Twelfth Night* in Pearson Park, on ground to the east of the conservatory, backed by an avenue of mature trees, a setting described by the Press as 'flowering fuchsias, green ferns and noble hydrangeas'. To its credit, for Hull was in the front line of the bombing raids, the City Council provided much support. The Parks Department built her a stage, together with scenery items which had to be collapsible. Often, the casts changed in Miss Drasdo's home and could be seen scurrying down the Avenue to the park. Crude benches and rickety park chairs were pressed into service to seat the audience, and the vagaries of the weather also played their part. The inexperience of wartime apprentice printers, too, resulted in such howlers as a poster advertising ' "The Drasdo" – a play by William Shakespeare.'

Geoffrey Bayldon, who went on after RAF service to take up a career in theatre and television, describes the very first production as 'having no electrified sound, only a wind-up gramophone and two 12-in records, all splendidly manipulated by Miss Geddes, Hannchen's great companion, behind a municipal bush'. He also recalls Hannchen's warmth and kindness, telling of her quietly taking him as a young boy under her wing and making him welcome in her home when he had to come to terms with the tragic loss of his mother in a motor accident. 'I loved every second under the Drasdo banner,' he says. 'And I loved Hannchen too. She had boundless energy and was larger than life and therefore twice as natural!' Many leading Hull amateurs supported Hannchen in these shows, as did Phyllis Sharrah, who was also involved in the Northern Command troop entertainment scheme. *The Merry Wives of Windsor*, with a notable Falstaff from the talented Sidney Carver, and *Twelfth Night* were followed by *A Midsummer Night's Dream, Toad of Toad Hall* – which played to throngs of children, even seated four-deep on the stage itself – *Much Ado About Nothing, Alice's Adventures*, with Mary Butterworth as an Alice straight out of a Tenniel drawing, and *The Comedy of Errors*.

Technical resources improved each year, and shows were usually staged in June and August to cover school holiday time. Latterly, shows were also given in Hull's East Park. In a lecture given to the Rotary Club, Hannchen stressed the need she felt for a purpose-built open air theatre in a park. Reviews, generous in the light of the rationing of newsprint, all comment on the high standards of the productions overall, including the effective costumes, but this was only to be expected when Hannchen had her hand on the tiller. A tough task mistress, she insisted on a wholehearted dedication from her cast; indeed, one very young aspiring actress was accepted only on condition that she ceased her tuition by another, less-approved, teacher of elocution!

Hannchen's brusque and didactic manner cloaked the warmest and most supportive attitude to her company, remembered by many others beside Geoffrey Bayldon, and she inspired fervent loyalty. Her most repeated phrase was the put-down, 'Oh my dear! You were positively *dire!*' Everyone worked hard to avoid that opprobrium. Her plays for the Forces, given over a wide area from the Wolds to gun-batteries at Spurn

Point and as far as Dishforth Aerodrome, were many and various. *A Murder has been Arranged* went down surprisingly well. The juvenile leading man recalls playing a scene in which he was attempting to seduce the heroine on a sofa when a stentorian voice on the Tannoy declaimed, 'It's now time for BLACK OUT!' Pandemonium ensued . . .

Ambrose Applejohn's Adventure, *The Two Mrs Carrolls* and *The Late Christopher Bean* were among many others cast – even if, on occasion, the leading man was somewhat youthful, all the over-18s having been called up. And the shows were well dressed in spite of rationing and clothing-coupons. Miss Drasdo found time in these exciting years to direct a 'Safety First Week' film for the local authorities, with a script by a local authoress, Miss H. C. Danby. This featured police and Fire Brigade services, and followed a popular 'family' type of story-line.

It was a loss to everyone when, at the close of the 1940s, Hannchen Drasdo was forced to bow to medical advice and restrict her activities. For many years she had struggled against asthma, but now the condition worsened. Nevertheless, Hannchen continued to take a lively interest in all matters theatrical, and to enjoy such of life's pleasures as were within her scope. Indeed, it was while quaffing a convivial glass of sherry that, in 1963, she suddenly died.

Drasdo Repertory Productions in Pearson Park

1942	*Twelfth Night*	
	The Merry Wives of Windsor	
1943	*A Midsummer Night's Dream*	
	Toad of Toad Hall	
1944	*Much Ado About Nothing*	
	Alice's Adventures	
1945	*As You Like It*	
	The Witch's Hat	(Muriel Roper-Spencer)
1946	*The Old Wives' Tale*	(George Peele)
	The Dark Lady of the Sonnets	
1947	*The Comedy of Errors*	
	Much Ado About Nothing	
1948	*Love's Labours Lost*	
	Toad of Toad Hall	
1949	*Lady Precious Stream*	
	A Midsummer Night's Dream	
1950	*The Merry Wives of Windsor*	(and at East Park)
	Tobias and the Angel	
1951	*The Taming of the Shrew*	(and at East Park)
	Alice's Adventures	
1952	*Twelfth Night*	

FUN FOR THE FORGOTTEN FORCES

By Sadie Ellerby

LARGE R.A.F. STATIONS and Army depots could rely on at least the occasional visit from the professional organisation, E.N.S.A., but the innumerable smaller units – searchlight batteries, anti-aircraft sites, anti-tank regiments, Royal Signals, Field Ambulance units and the like – could expect only voluntary entertainment, and we saw to it that in Hull and the surrounding area this was of a very high standard.

On 8 February 1940, the wartime Organisation for the Entertainment of the Services in Hull and the East Riding was set up at a meeting in the Guildhall, under the chairmanship of a local businessman, Cecil R. Jones, the head of Bladons Ltd, the Prospect Street store. Mr Jones, who became Honorary Entertainments Officer, Northern Command, headed an executive committee consisting of Mr Norman Pogson, secretary, Mr H. Atkinson, manager of the Midland Bank, treasurer, Councillor Wallace Rockett, Mr Austen Hudson, Mr W. S. Robinson, Miss Hannchen Drasdo and the Lady Mayoress and the Sheriff's Lady. The Lord Mayor, Councillor H. M. Harrison, was the President and the Sheriff was Vice-President. To assist with liaison between the organisation and the various units, Colonel Moss Blundell and Mr J. Ward, of the YPI, were elected, while on the production side were Miss Drasdo and Miss Phyllis Sharrah, along with representatives from Withernsea, Bridlington and Scarborough.

(Mr W. S. Robinson was the editor of the Hull Daily Mail, and a popular figure in the City, and Miss Peggy Shapero, the first columnist to turn the 'Miss Humber' feature from a mere title into a personality, was a leading figure among the entertainers – Ed.)

In due course, Northern Command set up an umbrella organisation to which all the local groups were affiliated – Voluntary Entertainment Service, Northern Command – its badge being a white rose. Northern Command awarded certificates to performers for every 100 performances. Three of the major amateur drama groups formed concert parties, The Charades (members of the Sharrah Drama Club), the Garrets (members of Hull Garret Players) and The Savoyards (members of the Savoyards Amateur Operatic and Dramatic Society). There were also The Gems, The Pals and The Mandarines, together with an accordion band led by Mrs Lottie Stubbins. In addition, a 1920s-30s concert party which had gone out of existence, The Vagabonds, was re-formed.

All parties had to be vetted before being allowed to perform, and the names of their members, all of whom had to be of British nationality, had to be registered with the parent organisation. Any new group had to pass an audition. An 'Entertainment for the Services Fund' was set up; although no artists were paid, transport, mainly by hired coaches, was expensive. Petrol coupons were provided by Northern Command. After about two years, however, buses were no longer available, and for a period we travelled in Army lorries, then by cars from the Volunteer Car Pool.

Often, when nearing Hull on our return journey, we would find an air-raid in progress. On many such occasions we would stop on the Beverley-Willerby road and look down on Hull to watch the raid. Though we were worried about our relatives at home, an air-raid viewed from that vantage-point was an awe-inspiring sight – the searchlights, the bomb explosions, the fires and the bursts of light and heavy ack-ack fire.

One incident annoyed us all: we were returning from a show given at Hotham Hall. The performance had gone down well, and we had been royally entertained to a magnificent supper in the Officers' Mess. It was one of the few occasions when we travelled in comfort in an East Yorkshire Motor Services bus, but, as we approached Beverley Market Place, the air-raid warning sounded. The driver parked his bus next to an air-raid shelter in the square, got out and went into the shelter, announcing as he left us that he would go no further until the All Clear sounded. There was not a sound of planes or gunfire, but we had to wait some two hours before the All Clear. We did not join the driver in the shelter but stayed in the bus and tried to get some sleep; I don't think the Air Raid Wardens were too happy about that, but we sat it out, nevertheless!

When we travelled by Army transport, the outward journey was simple enough, as the driver had only to find the school, or wherever the performance was to take place. On the return, however, we had to be dropped as near to our homes as possible. I don't know whether I really had a better knowledge of Hull than the others, but I was always the one told to travel with the driver. Had we been out north or west of Hull, this seemed sensible, since I would be the last to be dropped anyway, as I lived in East Hull. However, when we had been out east, towards the coast, which was quite often, I still did not have the pleasure of being home first, but had to guide the driver round the town and be dropped last.

We performed in village halls, village schools, aircraft hangars and under canvas. At Braffords Hall, the stage was made up of table tops. We coped until Ida Howard's toe-tap. The table tops moved, and suddenly one foot was trapped between them. She fell forward into the laps of the officers sitting on the front row, but fortunately she was not injured. After that, the toe-tap number was omitted when we had to play on such makeshift stages – but the matter was resolved a month or two later when Ida left us to join the A.T.S. Our only other exponent of toe-tap, Olga

Gardner, was temporarily away from Hull, otherwise they might have formed a toe-tap duet.

We gave a show in a huge marquee to a contingent camped in the middle of Bainton Woods. It had poured with rain for several days, and water dripped through the roof during the performance. To make matters worse, we had to change in nearby tents as there was no room to change in the performance marquee, and there was no cover as we ran back and forth to the dressing tents. Underfoot, it was a quagmire; the troops had laid duckboards but these were mud-covered and slippery. I don't think any of us actually fell in the mud, but there were some dicey moments. That company, however, had some of the best caterers in the Army, and they gave us a magnificent tea.

I shall never forget 15 September 1940. That Sunday we gave two concerts in the Village Hall at Middleton-on-the-Wolds for the R.A.M.C., with a break for tea. The Battle of Britain was at its height and the B.B.C. was broadcasting regular up-dates on the number of German planes shot down. The second concert was under way when the major in charge interrupted us to announce that it had just been reported on the radio that 115 German planes had been brought down. The audience went wild – we went wild! Everyone applauded and shouted and cheered. Some booze appeared from somewhere, but we hardly needed it; we were drunk with excitement. Phyllis even amended the programme so that we could include songs like *Lords of the Air* as a tribute to the R.A.F. Years later, of course, it came out that the number of planes had not been nearly so high as 115, but at the time it boosted everyone's morale.

Poor Eileen!
So many funny things happened. There was the camp where we were put into what we thought was an unoccupied barrack hut to get dressed. We thought all the bunks were empty, until the wolf-whistles started! Our soprano, Eileen Blake, always seemed to get the worst of things, especially at ack-ack sites. Once, when she was in the middle of *Shine Little Glowworm Glimmer*, a soldier walked in with a shovel full of coke which he put into the stove. The hut was filled with clouds of smoke. No-one could see a thing – the only light was from hurricane lamps – and poor Eileen choked and spluttered and had to retire.

Our show always opened with the full party, except for the dancers, seated in a semicircle, like the old pierrot troupes. We would go forward and do our number, then sit on our stools again to listen to the rest, or to watch the dancers, who generally did a fast tap routine at this point in the show. One night, we were halfway through this first part of the programme, and Eileen was nicely launched into her first number – on this occasion it was *Funiculi-Funicula* – when the air raid warning sounded. The wooden Army huts had a door at each end, and I suppose the boys were instructed to leave by the nearest door when they heard the warning. Those seated near the front charged across the stage and out of the door behind us, nearly knocking us over. Our silver stools went flying and the screens which we used to arrange across the rear of the stage as background in lieu of scenery were knocked over and trampled on. Before we got into the shelters, the guns had opened up. The boom of the 4.7s and the higher-pitched crack of the mobile 3.9s was deafening.

On our troop show journeys, Eileen always wore a round fur hat. Returning by bus from playing to the naval detachment at Spurn Point in the wee small hours, Eileen had her hat upside down on her knee. Before we left, the Navy had dosed us all with liberal tots of rum 'to keep out the cold'. Someone threw up, filling Eileen's hat. Thank goodness I can plead 'not guilty'. Poor Eileen!

On the outbreak of war, many societies abandoned their activities for the duration, but the Sharrah Drama Club was the first to get going again, and they not only presented *Dear Brutus* in November 1939, only a few weeks after the date originally planned, but also formed The Charades, which gave its first performance in the December of that year. By the end of January 1940, before the administrative organisation had even been set up, 12 shows had already been given to the troops. We often gave two shows a week, and we went out whatever the weather. We got stuck in snowdrifts and lost in the fog, and we travelled in every conceivable form of transport – buses, cars, tradesmen's vans and Army lorries. Setting off straight from work to a distant site, we often found it necessary to save time by changing and making-up en route, even in the back of a lorry with only a hurricane lamp to see by. We played at Spurn before the road to the Point had been built, and we had to travel on the Spurn Head Railway. These journeys were usually made in the Hudwell Clarke Railcar, although I believe we made one in a Hardy. I don't think the road was completed until early in 1941.

The Charades were scheduled to give a performance on the Hull Sand Fort, one of the massive island forts in the Humber Estuary, situated halfway between Spurn Head and Cleethorpes. Since the only means of reaching the fort was by boat, I was eagerly looking forward to it, but unfortunately our visit was cancelled because an E.N.S.A. party had been stranded on the fort for several days through a combination of bad weather and air-raids. Whether all-male parties – if there were any – were allowed to visit I don't know, but certainly after that stranding no females were allowed. It was late 1941, and from September that year we had been an all-female party, our men having been called up.

Flood alert
In addition to visiting the Forces, we gave performances in Hull to which Service men and women were invited. Venues included the Tivoli

Theatre, Mayfair Cinema, YPI Hall, City Hall – until bomb damage put a stop to this – and the Wenlock and Londesborough Barracks. Another adventure happened to us at the New Theatre in July 1941, during a very wet summer. The occasion was one of the V.E.S. Revues. The Charades were in the old No. 1 Dressing Room at the opposite end of the basement corridor running from the Stage Door under the scene dock, which had been bomb-wrecked in the May blitz. I remember receiving a frantic phone call from Phyllis Sharrah: 'Hurry to the theatre!' When I arrived, I found our costumes and props floating along the basement corridor; the heavy rain had poured into our dressing room, creating a minor flood. The next few hours were spent in retrieving our gear and carrying it up to the safety of the old Dressing Room 14 at the top of the building, some 70 steps up from the basement. But naturally, the show went on that evening.

Peppino Santangelo, General Administrator of the Little Theatre from 1933 and of the New Theatre from 1939, helped the work of the local V.E.S. Between 1941 and 1944, the V.E.S. mounted five different productions at the New Theatre, all under the direction of Phyllis Sharrah and each playing for one week, all the proceeds being devoted to Forces' charities. Local Services units were allocated a number of seats at each performance, and the shows took the form of either variety or revue. A lot of effort went into the planning of these productions to ensure that artists from all the concert parties were given equal opportunities for displaying their talents. The titles were, *V.E.S. Revue, Stars from the Troop Shows, Hello Hull V.E.S., Variety Highlights (V.E.S.)* and *The Show Goes On.*

I think a lot of the concert parties ceased their activities in 1945, but not the Charades. There were still a lot of Service personnel in the area, awaiting demob or in hospital, and, of course, there were many R.A.F. stations still operational and located near remote villages in Yorkshire and Lincolnshire. We began playing further afield, touring not only the concert party programme but some of our plays as well The V.E.S. continued until March 1947, when the organisation's last production, *1066 And All That,* again directed by Phyllis Sharrah, was mounted at the New Theatre.

Virtue, they say, is its own reward, but our efforts to bring high-quality cultural and comic relief for the fighting men and women in those small, isolated and often unglamorous units during those grim years, battling against the worst that the British weather and enemy action could do to us, did not go unrecognised, either among our audiences or from the Top Brass. A letter received in April 1940 from HQ Northern Command read: 'The schedule of entertainments given is an impressive one and I feel I must pay a special tribute to Hull for the wonderful work you are doing. The results are outstanding compared with any other part of the Command and I am very grateful to you.'

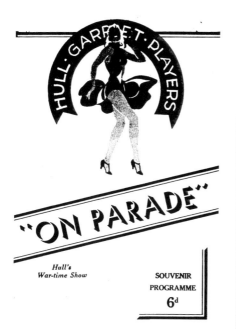

The Drasdo Rep. on tour.

The 'sound effects' department in the park operated by Miss Geddes.

The Drasdo Repertory Company in Much Ado About Nothing *in the park as part of the 'stay at home holiday' 1944*

32

THE LITTLE THEATRE MOVEMENT IN HULL, 1949-1955

THE FOLLOWING ARTICLE was written by Stella Sizer-Simpson shortly before her death on 7 May 1994.

For five glorious years, the Janus Theatre was home to the Sizer-Simpson Repertory Company which was founded in 1925 by Stella's mother, Isabel Sizer-Simpson, the principal of a Hull school of music and drama. On Isabel's retirement, her daughter, who had studied at the Guildhall School of Music and Drama in London, and had taught with several professional organisations, took over as director and producer. Stella was joined by her husband, the late Peter S. Harvey, as co-artistic director, and they had the support of Mrs F. Kirby-Hope as secretary and Miss M. Dowson as treasurer.

Between 1937 and 1939, the outline of the constitution was designed and the directors began to plan the policy which was eventually to give the company its own home. All productions were suspended between 1939 and 1944, but those members who were not called into the Forces or directed away from home continued to meet for play-readings and group activities in stage-craft. In 1945, with an increased membership, productions were resumed, and in order to give the younger members stage experience, a series of one-act plays was produced in Hull and the surrounding district. The year 1946 saw the return from the Forces of many of the more experienced members and the resumption of full-length plays.

After the closure of the Janus in 1955, Stella went on to direct many productions of light opera and musical comedy for the National Operatic and Dramatic Association, and her services as an adjudicator for the British Federation of Music Festivals and the Guild of Drama Adjudicators were in demand until shortly before her death. She served as an examiner for the English Speaking Board and the Poetry Society (London) for many years, and from 1965 she travelled extensively on behalf of Trinity College, London, conducting examinations and seminars in Canada, the U.S.A., Australia, New Zealand and Italy, as well as in the United Kingdom. She and her husband spent their retirement in Lincolnshire.

THE JANUS THEATRE

By Stella Sizer-Simpson

IT IS NOW some 35 years since the curtains closed on the last performance of the Janus Theatre, and, although memories of productions and acting members remain crisp and clear, dates and incidents have become lost in the mists of time.

When I was invited to contribute a chapter to this book based on the rise and fall of the Janus Theatre, I had to take recourse to diaries, Press cuttings, programmes and editorials to achieve a chronological order. On looking back at the original material, I felt that it conveyed much of the immediacy and emotional tone of the experience, and accordingly have included a number of extracts.

In common with other drama groups, we had great difficulty in finding a stage on which to mount productions, our earlier venue, the Royal Institution in Albion Street having been destroyed by enemy action. At that time, the Victoria Hall in the Boulevard was the largest stage available and it became our home until the building of the Janus Theatre. From 1947, drama courses were in being, and these formed a firm foundation for members when the theatre building was acquired.

Harry Hanson, of the Hanson Court Players, known locally for his pre-war season at the Palace Theatre, awarded an annual scholarship to the most outstanding member, with the opportunity of an audition at the conclusion of each year, should the recipient wish to enter the professional theatre. In consequence of this, John A. Corvin, the first holder of the scholarship, joined Mansfield Repertory and later moved on to Stratford; Paul R. Lamb was admitted to Drama College and later entered the teaching profession, becoming head of a large drama department; Anita Prynn was accepted at the Guildhall School in London and later worked in repertory and television; Hilary Walker commenced her career in Ilkley Repertory, and many other members became private teachers of speech and drama.

A Patronage Scheme was set up in 1944, and an editorial in our programme of *The Barretts of Wimpole Street* recorded its growth. In 1944 there were 15 active members and 10 patrons; by 1949 there were 112 active members and 75 patrons, while the mailing list had grown from 0 to 900! Our aims were set out clearly in a Newsletter sent to patrons and members in May 1949: 'Since the commencement of our post-war activities, the idea foremost in our minds has been to stimulate an appreciation of local dramatic talent, and from the support and encouragement received it is apparent that we have established ourselves as an integral part of the City's cultural life. Many difficulties have been encountered, the greatest of which has been the lack of a suitable venue. To remedy this, it has been decided to acquire a suitable building and to convert it into our own "Little Theatre". We realise, of course, the immensity of the task we are setting ourselves . . . '

The Newsletter went on to explain that our aims were the study and performance of plays which had an educational or entertainment value and were not usually performed in the commercial theatre, and to experiment in all forms of production and presentation, besides fostering an interest in the theatre, the principles of acting, the history of drama and other aspects of the art.

Such a project required both a capital outlay and an assured annual income, and to provide this security we devised and set out a membership scheme, stressing that the company was an association which existed solely for the promotion of its aims, and that no member or official received payment for his or her services: ACTIVE MEMBERS, whether actors, scenic artists, wardrobe mistresses, carpenters or electricians, were eligible to attend play readings and lectures and would pay a subscription of £1. 1s. per annum. PATRONS were entitled to book their seats two weeks in advance of the general public and to receive a copy of the quarterly Newletter and a free seat at each production, also for a subscription of £1. 1s. per annum. A list of patrons was included in each programme. ASSOCIATE MEMBERS, for a subscription of 5s per annum, had priority booking facilities one week in advance of the public and received a copy of the Newsletter. Subscribers automatically became members of the Green Room Club and were thereby entitled to use the Green Room and coffee bar.

Birth of the 'Janus'
In August 1949, the company was offered the leasehold of the Congregational Church on Hessle Road, Hull, and a number of members spent their vacation checking regulations and by-laws which had a bearing on our proposed conversion. On September 26, we started operations, the 'girls' and 'boys' working side by side, first removing the pews from the east and west transepts to make way for dressing-rooms, lavatories and the Green Room, and later removing the choir stalls, on the site of which we built the stage. All floors were levelled, a task which took nearly two months, and it was not until December that the entire site was cleared and we started building the interior walls.

Despite magnificent aid from our Honorary Architects, Bouch and Chapman, who drew up the plans, we experienced setbacks which at the time seemed insurmountable; and yet, one by one, each problem was solved and we were given the incentive to carry on. As a company, we prided ourselves on the fact that we had the courage of our convictions. Even so, our courage and capacity for work were relentlessly tested every day. Our band of workers diminished; some members felt that the creation of this theatre demanded too much of them, and in consequence the stalwarts who remained were given even heavier burdens to carry. Always, however, when the clouds were blackest there was a glimmer of sunshine – a donation, a gift of materials, encouraging letters from other clubs whom we had invited to become affiliated to the theatre . . . All of this strengthened our belief in what we were doing. Various firms allowed us credit, gave advice and assisted us in many ways.

During this period, some 5,000 letters and circulars were sent to the public, Press and notabilities of stage and screen. The costumes for our first production, *The Bluebird* – 83 in all – were also designed and made. The date of opening was postponed a number of times. We found it impossible to get materials through quickly enough, and work which should have been finished in January 1950 dragged on into the spring.

Meanwhile, our financial position was a source of real anxiety. When, on 21 April, we found that the theatre had been broken into by a group of youths who had wrecked equipment and effects and splashed paint over clothing and properties, our cup of woe was full. Nevertheless, we cleared the wreckage and started again, though with heavy hearts. At the following meeting of the Advisory Council, it was decided to open the theatre on June 10. We realised that it was necessary to mount a production to give us sufficient capital on which to work until our first full season began in September 1950. This was not an easy decision to make, for it must be realised that by this time all members were physically and mentally exhausted. In effect, it meant that the company had only four weeks to rehearse and build the sets for the opening production, and to organise the booking office and complete the building. However, with a deficit of £1,000 and running costs anticipated at £230 per annum, the Advisory Council felt it had no choice but to ask members to make this final effort.

For the technically minded, perhaps I should include here details of the theatre's dimensions and equipment. The stage measured 40 feet by 24 feet. It had a proscenium opening of 24 feet by 14 feet, a cyclorama, generous wing space and four traps. There was a grid with 18 lines and a flying height of 40 feet. The lighting equipment – two battens and one spot batten – consisted of four acting areas, eight spots, 16 floods, footlights and top and bottom lighting for the cyclorama. There were also eight F.O.H. spots. The 18-way interlocking dimmer-board was eventually replaced by a larger board. In the auditorium, the original pews, seating 250, were retained, 90 of the seats being in the balcony. At a later stage, banquette cushions were donated to the company by Councillor Frank Longstaffe. The Green Room and coffee bar were also used as additional rehearsal space. Dressing rooms and lavatories were constructed.

The Bluebird

On 10 June 1950, some eight months after the lease was signed, the theatre, as yet unnamed, opened with a production of Maeterlinck's *The Bluebird*. The official opening ceremony was performed by the Deputy Lord Mayor of Hull, Alderman J. Henson, and the play ran from 10 to 17 June inclusive, being directed and adapted by the co-directors. As well as local dignitaries, we had among our patrons some famous and respected theatrical personalities, including Yvonne Arnaud, Richard Attenborough and the Boulting Brothers, who sent letters expressing their good wishes and their belief in our venture. Some of these were reproduced in the original programme.

Harold Downs, editor of *Theatre and Stage*, wrote, 'The Little Theatre Movement as an integral part of the more comprehensive Amateur Movement was inevitable. Amateur activities that began as the expression of enthusiasm, combined with the desire and the determination to help forward any one of innumerable good causes, could not forever remain based on inadequate or unsuitable accommodation. From the beginning, however enthusiastic the amateurs and however laudable the incentives, there had to be development.' His assessment of my work was gratifying: 'Her standards are high, her methods exacting, her results outstanding. That the company is now in the fortunate position of being able to function in a theatre of its own is the reward of imaginative planning and methodical work. May it long be able to implement its aims.'

Peter Cotes, director of the Library Players, Manchester and London, wrote: 'Our country must produce writers of the paramount importance of Sean O'Casey, but, unless they have a platform upon which they may have their works performed, they will disappear. It is a theatre such as yours that must play its part in encouraging the type of dramatist who has something vital to say, and says it in an entertaining manner. By displaying that enthusiasm and encouraging the best of the new playwrights to write for a theatre such as yours, you will find your own reward, and I send my cordial greetings in the hope that you will stick to your guns by not lowering your artistic standards, thus keeping your original ideas intact.'

Shorter, but equally encouraging, was the contribution of Yvonne Arnaud: 'I am sure that you have the best wishes of all theatre-goers, and I wish you good plays, courage, patience and the determination to be successful.' And Richard Attenborough wrote that, 'this memorable occasion is the culmination of many years of hard work by Stella Sizer-Simpson and her Repertory Company and to them I wish every success and happiness in their new home. May the citizens of Hull give their long and continued support to this worthy project.'

These, and many other messages of warmth and goodwill, including one from the Queen (now the Queen Mother), encouraged us towards our first production. The local Press were kind to us, too. *The Hull Daily Mail* critic wrote, '*The Bluebird*, produced for the first time in its entirety outside London, revealed the greatest talent, well nurtured by the director, Stella Sizer-Simpson. The production was almost flawless and the delicate interpretation of the journey of two children into fantasy held the interest. It is a tale full of enchantment, with a constant change of scene, and the lighting effects lend moments of great beauty.'

We continued our first season with an ambitious programme of a further six productions, of which *Our Town* and *Dark of the Moon* were provincial 'firsts'. *Our Town* revealed Wilder's interest in Oriental dramatic forms, indicated by the spareness of the settings and the minimal use of properties. *Dark of the Moon*, a play built round the ballad of Barbara Allen, was presented as our Festival of Britain performance in lieu of our previous choice, Flecker's *Hassan*, the performing rights of which had been withdrawn because it was to be a theatrical feature of the London season.

Achieving a balance
We defined a major production as one which involved the majority of acting members, had multiple settings and period costumes, and was a classic of its kind. *The Bluebird, Our Town* and *Dark of the Moon* all came into this category.

Following our policy of sharing the theatre with other organisations, the company acted as hosts to the Festival of Britain, East Riding, One-Act Play Festival, held from 26 to 28 April, 1951. It must be borne in mind that the company's expressed aim was to present plays not usually performed in the commercial theatre, to experiment in all forms of production and presentation, and, at the same time, to produce a programme that would be sufficiently entertaining to appeal to the general public. Programme planning became a juggling act in which we attempted to balance the 'experimental' with the 'entertaining', and results indicated that we were reasonably successful in so doing. Patrons who sought entertainment were loyal in their support of more thoughtful productions, and those who were interested in experimental theate were equally supportive. The company brought the same dedication to every production. There was never a lowering of standard in settings, acting, direction or decor. Each production was as polished as our resources would allow.

During the theatre's closed season, July and August 1951, the co-directors were invited to apply for membership of the Little Theatre Guild of Great Britain. This entailed the presentation of two productions to be adjudicated by representatives from theatres affiliated to the Guild. A prerequisite of membership was that each company should have its own theatre. The programme for our second season was therefore built round two major productions, *The Lady's Not for Burning* and *Peer Gynt*, which were submitted for adjudication by the Guild. Thomas Walton, the chairman, and other members of Bradford Civic Theatre, attended the final performance of *The Lady's Not for Burning* and, as representatives of the Guild, adjudicated on the production.

For our third play of the season, Ibsen's *Peer Gynt*, we used the Norman Ginsbury translation. When it was first produced, the play was heralded as 'the most daring extravaganza of the modern theatre.' With a cast of 60 and 12 sets, this production presented the company with a major challenge. The Guild's team of adjudicators on this occasion was from the People's Theatre, Newcastle, under the chairmanship of Peter Trower. At the conclusion of the final performance, Peter Trower disclosed that he and Thomas Walton were recommending the Sizer-Simpson Repertory Company for full membership of the Little Theatre Guild of Great Britain. Subsequently, members of the company were invited to attend a meeting of the Guild at the Maddermarket Theatre in Norwich in May 1952, when they were formally welcomed as members.

It was at this stage that we introduced a season ticket scheme for patrons and associate members, to provide the company with additional income and an assured attendance. Contemporary photographs reveal excellent settings and lighting. The company's photographer, Eric Jackson, did not merely take pictures, he captured moments from the action, and the sets were a perfect foil for these vignettes.

My husband, Peter Harvey, designed the settings and painted them with the assistance of members, and I recall a number of occasions when he and I worked into the early hours to finish a set after dress rehearsal. The policeman on the beat was a regular caller for an early morning cuppa! I also recall that, after the dress rehearsal of *The Lady's Not for Burning*, Peter and I were both dissatisfied with the 'stone effect' of the medieval setting. After the members had gone, we re-painted the entire set, arriving home in time for breakfast and the day's work, after 36 hours in the theatre. But we were young then, and 'the play was the thing!'

The setting for *Arsenic and Old Lace*, our May 1952 production, was magnificently opulent with its stencilled 'wall-paper', handsome friezes, solid oak bannister rails and Victorian dressing. The cast, too, were well matched and experienced – great fun! This was followed by *The Eagle Has Two Heads*, the third of our major productions that season, and here the permanent setting was dominated by a central staircase and Gothic fireplace, handsome drapes and heavy oak furniture. Marjorie Boddy was an outstanding Queen, regal and dominant, and she spoke the structured dialogue admirably. But let the Press reports speak for themselves: Of *The Lady's Not for Burning*, the *Hull Daily Mail* said, 'Nothing of the play's magic was lost in the Sizer-Simpson Repertory Company's production and they handled the extravagant dialogue well. It was a clever, artistic production of Fry's musical jingle of theories, set in vaguely medieval times. The acting was of a sophisticated brand, and Fry's characters were imaginatively portrayed . . . Frank Williams played the disillusioned ex-soldier, Thomas Mendip, discoursing against the world and its ways with eloquence and vivacity. He used the stage extremely well and his performance was excellent. Playing the beautiful young woman accused of witchcraft, Jillian Oates was rather more volatile than previous interpreters of the role whom I have seen. She was captivating . . . '

Of *Peer Gynt*, the paper reported, 'The Sizer-Simpson Repertory Company in a short time have laid Hull playgoers under a heavy debt, a debt increased by their production of *Gynt* this week. Distinction is a rare quality these days. It is precisely this quality the production achieves, producer and players rising superbly to the challenge of a notably formidable play.'

Theatre Conference

At the close of our second season, I note that a reference was made to a substantial reduction of the capital debt. We opened our third season with a play that portrayed the very fabric of human drama – *I Remember Mama*. The action of the play presented many difficulties, and offered a challenge not often accepted in the amateur theatre. Multiple settings necessitated the use of boat trucks and the alternation of deep and shallow sets. We also needed an outstanding stage manager, and in Eric Gathercole, who had been with the theatre since *The Bluebird*, and also worked in the professional theatre, we had the right man.

Our second major production, *Othello*. proved to be very expensive, and a heavy drain on our finances, because the costumes we used were those worn in the previous year's London production. Indeed, Othello's sword was that brandished by Orson Welles. The setting, which consisted of a central flight of seven steps leading to a quayside and thence to a balcony, was a permanent feature. The flats on stage right were interchangeable to permit the suggestion of interiors. Heraldic drapes were used to mask the staircase when necessary.

The Phoenix Players were the guests of the company on 13 and 14 May 1953, with their production of *All for the Love of a Lady*, produced by Sidney Carver, and the month of June heralded the initial announcement that the company was to host a Theatre Conference on behalf of the Little Theatre Guild. The co-directors and the Advisory Council, recognising this as a signal honour and a momentous event in the history of the company, decided that the time had come to extend the role of the Council, which subsequently became the Management Committee under the chairmanship of Herbert Ward. The purpose of an extended committee was to reduce some of the burden of responsibility previously taken by the co-directors, who could then focus all their attention on the artistic side of productions and on programme planning. It also seemed appropriate that the theatre should at this time be formally named, and the name JANUS THEATRE was agreed. At the final performance of *Black Limelight*, the first production of the fourth season, the theatre was officially named, the ceremony being performed by Councillor Lt.-Colonel Rupert Alec-Smith.

A Newsletter issued in January 1954 informed patrons and members that 'The object of the Conference is to give delegates from the 21 member theatres an opportunity to see the work of the Janus Theatre, its planning, accommodation, scenic and lighting equipment, and, by attending a performance, to create an opportunity for critical discussion.'

The co-directors' first consideration was the selection of a play which would provide a challenge hitherto unaccepted by other organisations. Letters were exchanged between England and America, as a result of which the company was granted permission to perform the first amateur production of the Brian Hooker translation of *Cyrano de Bergerac*. The directors undertook the responsibility of mounting the play, which had five sets, 52 characters and 17th century costumes and decor. They also arranged accommodation for the 70 visiting delegates. The Conference was of such stature that civic support was sought, and this was granted. The organisation was immense, and the co-directors were grateful for the support of their chairman and committee. A souvenir programme was designed and illustrated by Frank Armstrong, an artist of distinction.

On Saturday, 27 February 1954, the delegates of the Guild were given a civic reception at the Guildhall by the Lord Mayor and Sheriff of Hull, and Herbert Ward chaired the proceedings. A business meeting of the Guild was followed by a performance of *Cyrano* and an on-stage buffet after the performance for delegates, patrons and members of the company. The Janus Theatre provided the venue for the Conference on the following day, when Dr L. due Garde Peach, of Great Hucklow Village Playhouse, opened the meeting with a talk on 'Showmanship in the Theatre'. This was followed by group discussions on various subjects ranging from 'An actor's preparation before first rehearsal' to 'Box Office publicity methods'.

Cyrano was followed by a well-supported production of *Alice in Wonderland*, and the children, who came in coach-loads, loved it. However, despite artistic successes, the financial problems which had always beset us, became insuperable. A newspaper report by 'Prompter' refers to the terms of our new lease: 'Trebled rent, higher electricity charges and licensing problems may mean a serious setback for this company unless all-season support is forthcoming.'

A Newsletter dated July 1954 contained the following: 'We should like to take this opportunity of thanking all those who regularly respond to our appeals for support. Without your help we could never have mounted

30 productions in the past four years, and it is to be regretted that despite this support the fortunes of the Janus are in such a precarious state. There has been a gradual falling off in receipts over the past months. Other companies, professional and amateur, have experienced the same problem during the past two seasons, and attribute this decline to the strong competition offered by television. As has been said, we are not the only company in this situation, but we can't afford to wait for the turning of the tide because we have no reserves. Since 1953 our running expenses have equalled our income, and we still have the balance of the original debt outstanding.'

It is perhaps a little ironic to recall, against this background of financial gloom, the glowing report in the *Hull Daily Mail* of the company's June production: *'Point of Departure*, by Jean Anouilh, is an artistic piece brilliantly interpreted and produced. In high-tension emotional roles, Frank Williams as Orpheus and Jillian Oates as Eurydice played their parts in a way little short of perfection.'

Because the financial problems could not be resolved, the co-directors, in August 1954, with the approval of the Management Committee, offered the option they held on the lease of the theatre to Hull Corporation. The theatre was offered in its entirety, complete with its expensive equipment. The only request was that the Corporation should become responsible for the payment of the remaining debt, some £300. The proposition was that the Janus should become a Civic Theatre, available not only to the Sizer-Simpson Repertory Company but to all other organisations wishing to avail themselves of its facilities. The Town Clerk, Mr E. H. Bullock, was sympathetic to the proposal, as were the chairman of the local Association of Drama Groups and his committee. However, it would need a majority decision of individual groups to decide the issue – and the fate of the theatre.

The *Hull Daily Mail* recorded that the Corporation's Parliamentary and General Purposes Committee had referred the matter to the Education Committee: 'Dramatic and cultural societies in Hull had been circularised to discover their reactions in the event of the Corporation deciding either to purchase or lease the theatre, said the Town Clerk . . . Broadly speaking, he added, the terms of replies showed that, though there was general approval of the principle, some societies already had their own facilities for putting on productions and did not wish to commit themselves to booking sessions at the theatre.'

At the beginning of the fifth season, the company had not received a tangible offer from the Corporation, so provision had to be made for the remaining three months of the lease. We opened what was to be our final season with a production of *The Show*, by Galsworthy, which was produced by Phyllis Sharrah and presented jointly by the resident company and the Sharrah Players.

During the theatre's closed season, the co-directors had adapted the script of a new play, *Fires on the Earth*, by Kevin Carroll ('Prompter' of the *Hull Daily Mail*), and this was given its première in October 1954. The play, which told the story of a young French nun who had seen a vision of the Sacred Heart of Christ, was also entered for the annual New Play Foyle Award, in which it won second prize.

Critic Maurice Horspool wrote: 'The first night of a new play is an adventure in which we all take part . . . The exquisite proportions and craftsmanship of Denis Simms' set made a worthy setting for Kevin Carroll's play. It is not easy to put real life on the stage because real life rarely follows an Aristotelian pattern in its drama. Here, the author has given us first and foremost a play. It is so framed that from its placid opening to its majestic close the action carries us on surely and inevitably to that moment touched with divine terror on which the final curtain falls . . . '

The Final Curtain

A production of *We Have Company* followed, and was directed by Frank Williams, one of our most valued members. This was his first production for the theatre, and we felt that the imagination he had shown with regard to choice of play and presentation augured well for the future. He had already proved his worth as an actor of great sensitivity, his more notable performances being Jordan in *Granite*, Cass in *Duet for Two Hands*, Preacher Haggler in *Dark of the Moon*, and Orpheus in *Point of Departure*. Frank was also to gain another distinction, though none of us recognised it at the time, in that *We Have Company* proved to be the last production to be presented at the Janus, and it was a fitting reflection of the work done and the standard achieved by the company during its five-year commitment to the art and craft of the theatre. Nothing, however, could delay the inevitable. The closure of the Janus was given headline prominence in the Press, and it was with a certain wry humour that we observed that we received almost as much publicity during its death throes as we did during our tenancy.

'JANUS SHOW UNREHEARSED, BUT OH SO MOVING!' ran the *Hull Daily Mail*'s headline in December 1954: 'They came to pick the theatrical "bones" of the Janus Theatre in Hessle Road today. There was no funeral oration, but is was obvious that the good of the Janus would live on after the interment. Faced with rising production costs, the Sizer-Simpson Repertory Company were selling up in an effort to clear their debts. They started £1,800 in the red, having converted a derelict church into one of the best amateur theatres in the country. But the hard work of six years was not enough to tip the scales to solvency . . . So the flats, tabs and other mysterious things that make paper characters larger than life were put up for sale today . . . Under the direction of Mr Gilbert Baitson, auctioneer, representatives from Hull University, school and drama groups moved eagerly from one pile of goods to another . . . The only theatre not represented was the Janus itself. As the auctioneer said sympathetically, "Perhaps they don't fancy coming to the funeral." '

'JANUS THEATRE CLEARS DEBTS WITH 2s. 5d IN THE KITTY' was the headline in March 1955, over a report by Kevin Carroll, wearing his 'Prompter' hat. He described it as 'a grand final curtain on the greatest and most courageous amateur drama experiment for many years. Now that it is all over, it is amazing the number of people who have expressed concern to me on the closing of the Janus . . . Mindful of its drawbacks, I can say with truth that the Janus Theatre fulfilled a noble mission. Over the past years it has been the scene of lively endeavour against dreadful odds. The playgoers of Hull from this venture shared many a glimpse of the greatness of the theatre. Members of the Sizer-Simpson Repertory Company can hold their heads high. They were a gallant lot, beaten only by circumstances that had little to do with their main achievements.'

Although now without a theatre, the company was invited by the Little Theatre Guild of Great Britain to continue as a member. This was a unanimous decision taken at a conference in Grimsby, where a delegate from the People's Theatre in Newcastle referred to the company as 'very valuable members'. And the 2s. 5d? This was placed in a charity box on the counter of Barclays Bank, where the final business of the company was completed.

Was the Janus a worth-while experience? Indeed, yes! And I am sure that if any member of the Repertory Company were to read this they would agree that, despite the worry and the stress, there was also an uplifting sense of achievement. We had done what we set out to do. We had fulfilled our aims, and we had never lowered our standards.

And what of the members? Many of them used the experience they had gained in the theatre as directors of, or actors in, other drama groups and Little Theatres elsewhere. Some entered drama schools and later made their way into the professional theatre or the teaching profession. And Peter and I? After a very brief rest we plunged into the world of the Operatic Societies, I as director, where I was later joined by other members who, with Peter, continued their stage activities in a different convention.

Did we make mistakes? Of course! But, under the pressures of the moment, our vision was blinkered and the mistakes unrecognised at the time. Though we, the co-directors, had a reasonably sound business acumen, we realise with hindsight that what the company really lacked from the inception was a strong Finance Committee, which would have been capable of dealing with the day-to-day business of the theatre. Had we been less idealistic, we should also have agreed the terms of the second lease before committing ourselves to the first. On the other hand, had we known that the terms of the second lease were to be so prohibitive, we would not have dared to open the theatre at all, and so would have missed the most exciting and artistically rewarding experience of our lives.

Stella Sizer-Simpson, Nettleham, Lincoln

List of productions

PRE-THEATRE PRODUCTIONS, 1946 to 1949

Tonight at Eight-Thirty	Coward	April	1946
Blithe Spirit	Coward	Oct.	1946
Death Takes a Holiday	Castella	April	1947
The Shining Hour	Winter	Nov.	1947
Berkeley Square	Balderston	April	1948
And So To Bed	Fagan	Nov.	1948
Miranda	Blackmore	Feb.	1949
The Barretts of Wimpole Street	Bazier	April	1949

FIRST SEASON'S PLAYS

The Bluebird	Maeterlinck	June	1950
Blithe Spirit	Coward	Sep.	1950
Our Town	Wilder	Nov.	1950
On Monday Next	King	Jan.	1951
Granite	Dane	Feb.	1951
Claudia	Franken	April	1951
Dark of the Moon	Richardson/Berney	June	1951

SECOND SEASON'S PLAYS

Death Takes a Holiday	Castella	Oct.	1951
The Lady's Not for Burning	Fry	Dec.	1951
Peer Gynt	Ibsen	Feb.	1952
Duet for Two Hands	Bell	March	1952
Young Wives' Tale	Jeans	April	1952
Arsenic and Old Lace	Kesselring	May	1952
The Eagle Has Two Heads	Cocteau	June	1952
Don't Listen Ladies	Guitry	July	1952

THIRD SEASON'S PLAYS

I Remember Mama	Van Druten	Oct.	1952
The Mad Woman of Chaillot	Giradoux	Dec.	1952
The Miser	Moliere	Jan.	1953
The Old Ladies	Walpole	March	1953
Othello	Shakespeare	April	1953

To Dorothy, a Son	MacDougal	May	1953
One Wild Oat	Sylvaine	June	1953

FOURTH SEASON'S PLAYS

Black Limelight	Sherry	Oct.	1953
Life with Father	Day	Nov.	1953
On Approval	Lonsdale	Dec.	1953
Cyrano de Bergerac	Rostand	Feb.	1954
Alice in Wonderland	L. Carroll	April	1954
Point of Departure	Anouilh	June	1954
Little Lambs Eat Ivy	Langley	July	1954

LAST SEASON'S PLAYS

The Show	Galsworthy	Sep.	1954
Fires on the Earth	K. Carroll	Oct.	1954
We Have Company	Gregg	Nov.	1954

Set and cast of Peer Gynt, *1952.*

Majorie Boddy as the Queen and Peter Harvey as Stanislas in Cocteau's The Eagle Has Two Heads, *June 1952. The set was designed by Peter Harvey*

A scene from The Lady's Not for Burning, *with Colin Mortimer and Jillian Oates, December, 1951.*

Valerie Benton, Jillian Oates and Edna Parry as they appeared in Alice in Wonderland, *April, 1954.*

Stella Sizer-Simpson and Peter Harvey (extreme right) surrounded by friends and well-wishers at the official naming of the Janus Theatre, October, 1953.

Picture *by courtesy of the* Hull Daily Mail

"The death of the Janus". The auction of the theatre equipment in December, 1954.

Picture *by courtesy of the* Hull Daily Mail

HULL GARRET PLAYERS

By Gillian Holtby

THIS IS a retrospective ragbag of personal memories, together with such facts as are still available, so I must explain a little about my early connections with the Society: Returning North in the late 1950s to pick up the work of an occupational therapist, I left behind me some years in the professional theatre, mainly in the commercially-based 'rep', both seasonal and touring, which had attempted for a couple of decades to revive the repertory theatre so popular before the war. This was a world of two plays a week on tour, of three 'houses' on Saturdays, and of scripts cut to ribbons when the cast needed to scramble on to the last London-bound train home . . . but that is another story.

Those returning from wartime service, or whose drama school courses, like mine, had been cut short by 'call-up', found working opportunities few and far between, with unscrupulous managements ever ready to cut corners in casting, eking out the Equity-minimum assistant stage managers with eager amateurs. Such a climate did not create a favourable impression of the amateur world with those who were at that time fighting for a livelihood. Later, I was to learn of the talent and dedication in the ranks of the amateurs, but at that time I was wary, and disinclined to become involved.

However, through Miss Hannchen Drasdo, to whom a family friend introduced me, I was approached by the Hull Garret Players, who were currently rehearsing a play in which the producer had perforce to play the leading role himself. Could I help him out? I went along in two minds, and sat, well in the background, to listen. Then, that instinct which pushes one into theatre direction – the joy of seeing the development of those dimensions only tangentially obvious on the scripted page, and of working with an actor in realising his potential – began to nag, and I was committed.

Later, I learned something of the Society's earlier history: In July 1934, a group of young people, dissatisfied, as always, with the opportunities offered to them by their current societies – mainly the Playgoers and the Sharrah Drama Club – formed a new, and in some respects complementary group (for several retained dual membership), The Rhodian Readers, under the presidency of Mr E. Rhodes. Two of their aims, as stated in the minutes, give, perhaps, some rationale to the group's formation:

1. Encouragement of all original work, prose, poetry or plays.
2. No cliques to be allowed among members (!)

In 1936 it was decided to re-name the group to avoid too personal an identification, and, as the meeting took place on the top storey of the Church Institute, the Garret Players came into being. Little material survives concerning the pre-war productions, but Press cuttings record that, along with members of other societies, 'Garret' members were used by the management of the Little Theatre on a number of occasions when plays required a large cast.

In 1939, there were indications of the scene developing in Europe, In that year, profits from productions were given to the Refugee Fund, and the tenancy agreement for new meeting premises at 177, Anlaby Road, contained a clause requiring immediate termination of the agreement in the case of a 'national emergency'. The emergency was not long in coming, and all rehearsals were suspended. Membership fragmented, but the small nucleus which remained, spurred on by Stan Williscroft, immediately formed a sub-committee to organise variety shows for the entertainment of the troops and supportive communities.

The end of the war found Stan Williscroft in the professional theatre. As the *Hull Daily Mail* later recorded, 'When W. Stanley Willis-Croft left his desk at Hull Corporation Electricity Department to join the R.A.F., he could have had no idea that ten years later he would be producing well-known stars in the West End.' The Society, whose scenery and props had been 'blitzed', met again to review the post-war situation. Names from the earlier days were still prominent – Oliver Webb, Marjorie Aaron, Kathleen Caley, Harry Christian, Margaret Ramskir and others. One immediate problem to be faced was production premises; in 1947, the Garrets became affiliated to the Kingston upon Hull Citizens Arts League, and, like other groups at that time no doubt, echoed the statement in the League's advisory pamphlet, ' . . . those who have to arrange public concerts, theatre performances and public lectures are all aware of the almost heart-breaking difficulties that are encountered'.

Work in the Proscenium
Production in the early 1950s followed an 'on-off-on' pattern. Oliver Webb was an able producer, in addition to his artistic abilities in costume design, set design and painting, prop-making and the teaching of the art of make-up, but he had commitments at home, due to his wife's illness. Nevertheless, productions were mounted at the Holy Trinity Church Hall and the Co-operative Hall in Kingston Square. His 1955 production of François Mauriac's *Asmodee* introduced a very young Madeline Blakeney, later to become a successful professional actress, and first brought forward the juvenile Richard Green, who was later to contribute so much to amateur drama in the city.

The first Garret production I was invited to direct, Anouilh's *Waltz of the loreadors*, was also my introduction to the competitive festival. My feelings on this were equivocal: as in so many other fields – noticeably the sporting world – the worst and the best can be drawn out in competing teams. However, the Scarborough-based Yorkshire Drama Festival was the occasion of my meeting with that excellent adjudicator, the late Stephen Joseph, the pioneer, through his Studio Theatre, of alternatives to the proscenium theatre. A Cambridge M.A. and a graduate of Iowa University, he lectured, taught and dedicated his life to the development of an 'actor's theatre – in-the-round.' He was a charismatic figure, and I remember his guidance and friendship with gratitude.

The staging problems I had noted when first 'sitting in' on a Garret production at the Farmery Hall in Hull were very real. The stage was, in fact, simply a rather high platform, with appalling sight-lines from the floor of the hall, and totally inadequate lighting. Added to this was the impossibility of any technical rehearsal before the inevitable one-and-only dress rehearsal. A confusing back-stage layout, leading to one actress finding herself in the middle of a Transport and General Workers Union meeting when she had assumed that she would be stepping out into the wings, did not help matters!

It says much for Ron Kay, Alex Scotland, Alan Neave and the others that, during our use of this hall, lighting pylons were obtained, transported and marshalled into position to provide the front-of-house lighting, miles of cable were brought in, lamps hired (or borrowed) and slung, and a sound-system achieved. No wonder a photograph of one dress rehearsal catches the cast desperately tucking into fish and chips, conscious that business will extend into the small hours. The old hands accepted this as the status quo, but youthful enlistments, under the stricter parental control of the time, had some difficulties in convincing their families of the necessity. 'Is the woman mad?' stormed Gilbert Shipham's father the night before that young actor's debut. The producer's shoulders needed to be broad.

In *Lady from the Sea*, I worked for the first time with Oliver Webb as set designer, and enjoyed the consultations he initiated and the immaculate and detailed model set that he built, which was a real bonus in demonstrating to casts the conditions they would not have the opportunity to meet in reality until the dress rehearsal. Yet, although it was well staged, with excellent central performances from Ted Tilley (for so many years the backbone of the Society) and from the delightful Dorothy Cawthorn, the production did not make a profit. For many years – until it was capped by losses more momentous – Oliver and I were dogged by the minutes recording concern at the 'very huge loss'. The actual figure? Twenty pounds!

Though I acknowledged the concern, and recognised that jumble sales, raffles and social events must go on to make good a debit balance, I wanted the members to take on a more challenging production, one that would stretch their collective skills to a new level. And a challenge presented itself when, being interested in the Brechtian theatre and looking for a text I thought would be within the group's abilities, I found *The Visions of Simone Machard*. This had had a single performance in this country, to a club membership only, and it was difficult to obtain the text; printed copies did not exist. It had not yet, in fact, received the Lord Chamberlain's licence for public performance. The score of the incidental music, composed specially for the play by Hans Eisler, had to be obtained in rudimentary form on film from Germany, and needed to be completely scored and arranged for musicians to record. The work was considerable and the cost more than the Society's available budget. The Company of the Way were therefore invited to stage a joint production with us, and a happy co-operative it became.

Negotiations were conducted with the Lord Chamberlain (who objected to the use of the word 'arse'!) Sterling work on the part of Hull Philharmonic Orchestra under Geoffrey Heald-Smith brought the Eisler music to life. Then came slave-driving rehearsals at which, for the first time, I realised the potential of using a whistle when faced with the organisation of an angry mob. George Appleyard and Robert Barrett achieved the near-impossible back-stage, given that in the Farmery Hall they were working virtually blind in cueing-in.

Finally, the parable of a little peasant girl who acts out her identification with Joan of Arc in the face of the German Occupation reached the stage. It was a compliment to the whole company to read in the *Manchester Guardian*, 'Suzanne Robinson has an electrifying moment. . . She sinks to her knees and hammers the earth of France to awaken the land, and Eisler's great atonal drum-beats fill the hall. This is Brecht's Epic Theatre, and, in one untheatrical and uncritical word, WOW!' A postscript to this production, received some time afterwards, was a letter signed by Helene Weigel, inviting us to send production data for the Berthold Brecht Archives. Another was the discovery, some four years later, that a Manchester theatre club was claiming the first public production of *Visions*. This could not be allowed to go unchallenged, and, as our licence in 1963 from the Lord Chamberlain read, ' . . . allow the performance of a new stage play', our evidence was conclusive.

The Farmery Hall was last used by us in 1967 for Muriel Spark's *Doctors of Philosophy*. Then, following the use of a large number of Garret members in a 'Town-and-Gown' production of Giradoux' *The Enchanted*, which I also directed at the University's Middleton Hall, against an excellent set by Oliver Webb, it was decided that Oliver's production of Vanburgh's *The Confederacy* should also go on at the same venue, although this is a stage that I feel does not easily lend itself to drama. The wide proscenium and flat 'orchestra' area require sets that can convincingly bring down the scale of the stage and, with tasteful lighting, focus the audience's attention. Looking recently at a set of Oliver's costume designs for that play, I remembered the extent of the work that went into their making. Yard after yard of unbleached calico was dyed at home to his chosen palette and made up by his indefatigable wife, Molly, and others.

The Library Theatre was first used by the Garrets in 1972 to stage, with an extended company under the direction of Richard Green, the first of his two productions of *Cabaret*. The second, under the Northern Theatre Company banner, took place at the New Theatre and was on a larger scale. A full-length musical was a new and demanding venture. With the dual responsibility of directing and also playing the sinister 'Emcee', the pressures on Richard were considerable, as were those on his technical director, Bryan Williams, but the excellence of the production team which had been assembled, and the work of both members and those who had been invited to join us, ensured that the show resulted in a sell-out success. A personal memory is of standing motionless on the stage for a full 20 minutes before the show began, staring out into the auditorium while one by one the others in the cast filtered on to join me, also posed and still. This was an uncanny experience, and it had the effect of quelling completely the usual pre-curtain chatter of an assembling audience. Tony Cook, who was later to turn professional as 'Tony Mandel', and Ann Carter gave delightful performances in the 'Isherwood' role and as Sally.

At last, in 1970, the Garrets achieved their ambition to mount a Shakespeare play, something which a number of members had found particularly rewarding when working during the war with Hannchen Drasdo. *Twelfth Night*, directed by Maureen Marshall, went on at the Middleton Hall with Susan Uebel as Olivia, Ann Carter as Viola, and an excellent Feste from Arthur Winstanley, who gained praise from the Press for providing 'some of the most satisfying scenes in the play'.

From the expanse of the Middleton Hall to the confined, low-ceilinged Library Theatre, with all its disadvantages of lack of wing space and back-stage facilities, demanded an entirely different directorial approach, but change of tactics was by now par for the course for a Garret director, and for the back-stage crew. At least the Library audience enjoyed their creature comforts, even if the embarrassment of sharing a 'loo' with the audience made for interval problems among the cast! It also provided a different ambience from that of the 'Farmery', where, responding to the complaints of members, 250 cushion pads were made in one week to alleviate the discomfort caused by the stacking-chairs.

It was with considerable pleasure that, in 1973, Ian Hey took Brecht's *Mother Courage* into the Spring Street Theatre for the Garrets. For the first time, full lighting rig was allied to manageable dimensions of staging area, plus a central location – and a bar! The production received welcome financial support from the Lincolnshire and Humberside Arts, or it would not have been possible to stage the play, having regard to the company's finances. But Spring Street was seldom available at the required time of year, and a further seven productions went on at the Library. The last, *Play it Again Sam*, was mounted in the simplest form, using a long rostra, two short flights of steps and a screen which enjoyed the unifying factor of three large facsimile 'Bogart' film posters, reproduced by Oliver Webb. I was pleased that in this, my last full-length production for the Garrets, Oliver's skills were as integral as they had been in the first.

In the Round
The Theatre-in-the-Round work that Stephen Joseph was doing at Scarborough made it apparent that here was the opportunity for our members to work across the year, not just towards an annual production. Many of the staging problems inherent in the 'Farmery' could be avoided, and there would be opportunities for emergent directors and actors to try their wings. But where? Finally, the Garrets resolved to use the meeting-room on the ground floor of the Church Institute, in the attics of which the Society had, over the years, given fortnightly play-readings. The big room was lit by 'institutional' green enamelled glass-shaded pendant lamps on frayed flex, and the dull ochre and chocolate-brown paint was not in its first youth. But at least the state of the linoleum absolved us from too nice a conscience as we dragged in skips and lighting-pylons. The pillars in one area made it essential to confine our acting 'auditorium' to a 12-foot square of floor defined by adhesive tape and surrounded by two or three rows of bentwood chairs. A further row was raised upon the little lecture platform, and exits and entrances were confined to the diagonal corner aisles. Thus, the old Subscription Library, as it had once been, took on a new lease of life that was to run for five years. It was rough and ready in the extreme, but it certainly captured public attention. It did not entirely please the critics but, for good or ill, this was all grist to the mill of necessary publicity.

From the start, Stephen Joseph gave advice and support, and, when we mounted our first in-the-round programme in Hull, he loaned us an exhibition of material on the subject for the interest of the audience. He actually came to see the production twice.

The plays chosen, Ionesco's *The Bald Prima Donna* and *The Art of Making Friends*, by Charles Vildrac, provided further matter for the sharpened pens of critics. The Theatre of the Absurd had little appeal for the average smaller amateur groups in the provinces at that time, yet the genre contained many opportunities for widely-differing interpretations, and, at best, could pack such a theatrical punch that I was not surprised when Muriel Crane, the Staff Tutor in Drama at Hull University, in a letter to the *Hull Daily Mail* after their headline, 'Words . . . words . . . words . . . ', wrote, 'The play really seized the audience in a way I have

54

rarely known in even a professional performance today. Their enthusiasm expressed itself with a 19th century fervour.'

The alchemy that my cast, headed by the late Betty Rowland, with Alan Coates, Arthur Winstanley, Margaret Neave, Dorothea Desforges and George Appleyard, created for me was rewarded when, in his 1967 publication, *Theatre In The Round*, Stephen Joseph gave us a very complimentary paragraph on *The Bald Prima Donna*. Other in-the-round programmes followed, and the directors, Oliver Webb, Dennis Simms, Peter Shaw, Maureen Marshall and myself, will all remember the old 'Institute' for different reasons. In my memory's scrap-book are the partnership of George Appleyard and Arthur Winstanley in *The Bespoke Overcoat*, and the pleasure of directing, in *Professor Taranne*, a young Newland High School girl, talented, eager and responsive, now known to millions through television and theatre as Maureen Lipman.

The Garret Studio Theatre

The year 1967-68 saw the start of a period in the 'Garret Experience' to which all who were members at the time look back with interest and affection. This involved the conversion of two rooms on the ground floor of a high, double-fronted 'Avenues' house into the Garret Studio Theatre, in which it was hoped to mount trial productions of 'non-commercial' works, hold readings and social events, and enable members to engage in even more productions in one season than had been possible with only the Institute as an alternative to costly renting.

Dennis Simms and Peter Shaw had made their home in one of two ground-floor flats in the house, and the other, with amazing generosity – verging, some might think, on the foolhardy – was made available to the Garrets at a peppercorn rent. Dennis and Peter not only agreed to the essential initial step of throwing the two rooms into one rectangular area, but superintended the installation of the necessary heavy steel joist and a number of other modifications. Dennis, who had long been known in the amateur theatre in Hull and district as a practical man of the theatre, and Peter, who had had many years of experience of acting and directing with a number of local companies, worked hard with a nucleus of Garret members to give a new guise to their spare ground-floor flat, thereby sacrificing the tenant it might have attracted.

An overall stage area of only 12-feet by 14-feet, giving an acting area of 12 x 8, with one sole entrance up-stage left, created problems for director, technicians, designer – and cast. Much ingenuity was shown in creating small, masked areas in which an actor could 'freeze' off stage, unable to move until the next entrance cue. A tiny room, initially the kitchen, provided the only 'back-stage' area in which the cast could assemble. At the outset, relying on the hospitality of the two owners, the cast dressed on the premises and then, at the three-minute call, went through the yard and climbed through a sash-window in the rear wall of the 'theatre' to gain a back-stage location. What had been a cupboard flanking the chimney-breast eventually contained the switchboard and tape-deck, with the stage staff perched owl-like in isolation for the duration of the show, but Bob Witty and Stewart Ward, who laboured to fit up the theatre and to give technical support, displayed the necessary fortitude! Rostra were installed to rake the 12-foot by 14-foot auditorium, which seated almost 60 on an assortment of chairs.

The Garrets mounted a number of shows with a surprising sophistication of setting for such conditions. For one early full-length play – Dennis's production of *The Old Ladies* – he even achieved an inset behind gauze, in which, as Agatha, I brooded in my rocking chair, praying that it would not shift off the rostrum and precipitate me on to the ankles of the audience, only a yard away. We were pleased at this time to mount the 'amateur premiere' of Alan Plater's *The What on the Landing,* together with a seven-part anthology of his poems, stories and sketches, directed by Elizabeth Daniels under the title of 'Plater Playhouse'. The *Hull Daily Mail,* commenting on the fact that the Garret Studio necessarily played to an invited audience, remarked, 'Anyone who can beg, borrow or steal an invitation to "Plater Playhouse" should do so at once.' Payment was requested for refreshments only, and a large slice of the modest proceeds went to Alan Plater's nominated charity, the Hull Arts Centre Appeal.

The busy years at the Garret Studio saw a wide range of dramatic productions, from Ibsen, Maugham and Coward to the more contemporary Terson, Schaffer and Neil Simon. The confined space and 'club' atmosphere created an attraction of its own, and word-of-mouth publicity attested by audience attendance indicated the pleasure created. But the very extent of the work undertaken meant that a heavy burden fell on the small group able and willing to give technical support. Problems in both management – how to drum up volunteers for the regular sessions of cleaning and maintenance essential to our tenancy – and the effect of the political climate of the time created a difficult situation. In one of the inevitable power-cuts, a studio production managed to continue with rows of candles and night-lights in jars and on saucers, backed by kitchen foil! It was enough to make a risk-conscious stage manager have a seizure, but at the time it seemed preferable to turning 60 people out into the blacked-out streets.

With costs escalating, it seemed more and more selfish to occupy premises which had originally been intended as a spacious flat, and for which the Society was in no position to offer rental at the market value. It was clearly time to draw the Studio episode to a close.

EPILOGUE

DURING THE CLOSING years of the 1970s, the Garrets encountered many problems. Seeking a venue for in-the-round, they tried first a church hall in Freehold Street and then premises which had been converted from an old school into a community centre. Neither proved satisfactory. Shortage of scenery and props had made things progressively more difficult and much had had to go. The extensive wardrobe, painstakingly built up and managed, was housed for a time in archaic church school buildings in Dansom Lane, but it had been vandalised. Technical support was particularly difficult, though Ronald Kay worked for the Society to the limit of his abilities throughout. With the change in climate for amateur actors, old society identification was giving way to casting by invitation across a wide pool of known local theatrically-experienced people regardless of membership, and the administrative core of the Society was considerably reduced.

During the years I had worked with the Garrets I had always thought it inappropriate that I should serve as President. Directing was the best contribution I could make for the group's welfare; but now, with depleted membership, the argument was put to me that I might create confidence by accepting the Presidency, and I agreed at last to stand. However, when the annual meeting arrived, attendance was so poor that a committee could not be formed. Greatly disappointed, the small cluster of members discussed the situation. It was decid᷄ 1, in accordance with the rules of the Society, to call an Extraordinary General Meeting and to inform members beforehand of the importance of the occasion in an attempt to rally support.

When the meeting took place, most of us were in two minds. Our hearts were seeking a future for the Garrets, but in the main we knew that the changing times were against us. Better, I felt, to finish cleanly than to peter out with progressively less satisfying work. This is why, when the motion was proposed by a long-standing member that the Garret Players should be wound up, I felt I must, with considerable distress, support the motion, which was carried by a majority vote, despite the tear-bright eyes of at least one elderly founder-member.

The Garret chapter thereupon closed – and I never did get to wear that beautiful chain of office . . .

TAKE BACK YOUR FREEDOM

IN OCTOBER 1985, the 50th anniversary of the death of Winifred Holtby was commemorated by a production at the Library Theatre of the only published play by the East Yorkshire novelist, journalist and political campaigner, Take Back Your Freedom.

The play had been taken up for production by Tyrone Guthrie and amendments were discussed shortly before the author's untimely death. A version considerably amended and edited by Norman Ginsbury was staged in 1940.

Ironically, the emergence of dictatorship that she had dramatised had by then been overtaken by events; the play could have no future. As a kinswoman of Winifred (second cousin once removed, to be exact) Gillian Holtby had been anxious to learn to what extent the script had been re-written, and to compare the actual manuscript with the published text, with reservations as to many of the changes. However, Vera Brittain, as Winifred's literary executor, had conferred all rights on Norman Ginsbury, and, with Gillian's own cutting and some re-editing from Winifred's original text, his version was produced at the Library Theatre. Mr Ginsbury, who has since died, attended the final performance.

The commemorative nature of the production was underlined with Winifred's verses, No Mourning, By Request, *spoken by Gillian Holtby as an epilogue. – Ed.*

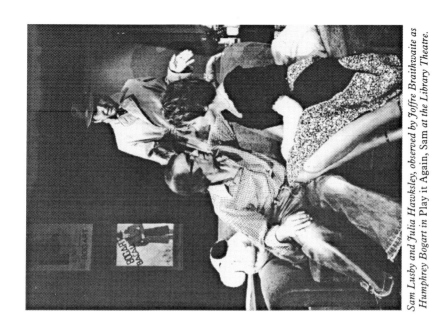

Sam Lusby and Julia Hawksley, observed by Joffre Braithwaite as Humphrey Bogart in Play it Again, Sam at the Library Theatre.

The Hull Theatre Group, an amalgamation of 'Town and Gown', gave a number of productions in the late 1960s. Picture shows Exit the King, by Ionescu, in which 'Gown' was represented by the King (Michael Walton), 'Town' by the Elder Queen (Gillian Holtby), and the students by the Younger Queen (Gillian Osborne). The designs were by Oliver Webb.

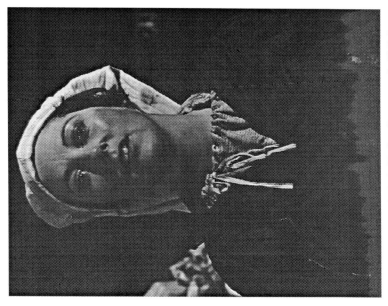

Lenore Showler as Katrin in Mother Courage at the Hull Arts Centre, now Spring Street Theatre, in 1973.

Suzanae Robinson as 'St. Joan' in The Visions of Simone Marchard by Berthold Brecht. Freda Hobson and Margot Blancheri are the masked nuns. Presented at the Farmery Hall in 1963 in a co-production with the Company of the Way, this was the first public production of the play in this country.

Theatre-in-the-Round in the Church Institute, 1960-61 season. Dorothy Cawthorne, Edward Tilley and Arthur Winstanley in The Art of Making friends.

Alan Plater discusses The What on the Landing *with Alan Neave, Gillian Holtby, Dorothea Desforges and Arthur Winstanley in the small studio theatre in Westbourne Avenue, 1968.*

THE 'CRIT'

By Barbara Robinson

THE MEMORIES had faded, and what remained merged into a jumble of half-forgotten impressions . . . but reading Stella Sizer-Simpson's account of the rise and fall of the Janus Theatre brought to the surface incidents from my life as a music and theatre reporter for the *Hull Daily Mail* which I thought had gone beyond recall.

It was really my interest in show-business that projected me into journalism. While still working as a secretary in the newspaper office, I would stand at the News Editor's elbow as he dished out 'night jobs' from the diary. There were never enough duty-reporters to cope with the multitude of events we were requested to cover, so some of the bits and pieces came my way – films at second-rate cinemas, amateur shows, school productions, things that the 'proper journalists' did not consider worthy of their steel. In those halcyon days, local newspapers attempted to respond to as many requests for coverage as they possibly could, and, although we could not please everyone, the result was a pretty good picture of what was going on in the area, regardless of whether it came under the heading of hard news or of simple reportage of events 'because they happened'. The *Hull Daily Mail* was particularly good in this respect.

There was no closed shop in journalism, and, when I later joined a union, I always voted against any such restriction, remembering that if one had been in operation at the time, I, and many like me, could never have got into this rather peculiar profession. As time went on, it was apparently recognised that I had a penchant for this kind of work, and besides, with, alas, no family life or romantic entanglements to distract me, I didn't mind how many night jobs I took on. I began to get more important assignments, covering the more prestigious amateur and college productions, and, eventually, the New Theatre.

There seems to be a strange impression in some quarters that we were not allowed to criticise the professional theatre. That was not true. Editor Tom MacKim, in particular, would defend to the death the right of his reporters to give fair and unbiased reviews of any show. What happened was that at certain times the theatre management, especially that doyen of administrators, Peppino Santangelo, felt that the role of the local Press was to support the struggling professional theatre at all costs, and never to publish anything which could discourage patrons from attending the performance. There were many epistolary battles between the Editor and Peppino – I know because I typed a lot of the letters – but they were mostly in the nature of brilliant literary fencing, and, out of the gymnasium, as it were, the two were firm friends, with, I believe, a great respect for each other.

I was luckier than some of my critical predecessors, because, by the time I came to occupy the regular Monday night Press seat at the theatre, Bill Sharpe had become the manager, a charming man with an equally charming wife. Bill took a reasonable line about criticism, and I for my part usually managed to indicate in my 'crit' that 'if you like this kind of thing, this is the kind of thing you like!' I sometimes felt that the City's more erudite drama teachers and producers of the time were rather unkind to Bill and the 'New', not appreciating the difficulties of booking good shows for a theatre which could not guarantee good audiences, at a time when television was drawing more and more regular patrons away from live entertainment.

During this period, the *Hull Daily Mail's* companion weekly newspaper, the *Hull Times*, ran a regular feature, 'In Town This Week', which involved interviewing the leading lights from the show. I enjoyed this tremendously, as it gave me a chance to meet many of the top entertainers of the day. Some of the older ones, such as Robertson Hare and Renee Houston, had great stories to tell of the legendary figures of the past, and were extremely articulate and communicative off stage as well as on stage; but with many of the more recent comers to the profession, I came up against the plea, 'Look luvvy, I'm just a working actor . . . ' And I feel sorry for many of today's popular magazine writers who seem to have to spend so much time trying to weave spicy and exciting features around the soap stars of the present day.

It was not the professional actors but the amateurs who were the most resentful of criticism. If one failed to mention each and every player or musician and give him or her a pat on the back, one got an earful over the telephone the next day. I once wrote a glowing review of a production of *Oklahoma!* in which every single member of the huge cast was named – dancers, chorus, the lot – but I failed to distinguish the dream ballet sequence from the overall production numbers – and there was hell to pay!

Drama in Education

School productions gave me particular pleasure, and I have special memories of Kingston High School where, under the direction of John Large, actors such as Tom Courtenay and John Alderton were nurtured and encouraged, and ambitious Shakespearean and other classical productions undertaken. I also had the privilege of seeing Maureen Lipman take her first stage steps at Newland High School, and later of following, with pleasure but not surprise, her rise to fame.

Similarly memorable were some of the Hymers College plays, in which the producer manfully – an apt term – overcame the problem of having to cast boys in female roles. We know that this was the norm in classical times, but some of the modern plays chosen, such as Galsworthy's *Strife*, were a different kettle of fish. Riley High School turned a necessity into a virtue by putting on a series of Gilbert and Sullivan comic operas – great fun! The school had some excellent boy sopranos at the time, and, quite frankly, the 'sisters, cousins and aunts' looked prettier than girls. A colleague, who was also an artist, pointed out that young boys, when dressed and made up as girls, did tend to look better on stage than girls of the same age, because male features were already more distinctly formed. Perhaps this is one reason why they were used in the early theatre?

I must mention, too, the pioneering work of Kelvin High School in introducing what were then unconventional art-forms in schools, such as dance-drama. And it was there that I saw my funniest-ever production of *Charley's Aunt,* with a wonderful scene in which 'Auntie', black bombazine skirts flying, rode a bicycle through the auditorium. There were many other schools, including St Mary's and Hull Grammar School, which tackled really ambitious musical and dramatic works with amazing success, and I wish there were space to list more of them.

Village shows
That must truly have been the golden age of amateur drama in Hull and district. Almost every commercial company had its drama group – we even had one at the *Hull Daily Mail* for a brief spell, though I don't think the management were very keen on it. It was not a success – my fellow thespians seemed incapable of learning lines, for a start – and it didn't last long.

Village shows were often, in themselves, a delight, but getting there and back was frequently a nightmare. Reporters were not provided with cars in those days, and, unless one was accompanying a photographer, who had to have a vehicle in which to carry all his gear, including a supply of flash-bulbs, one had to use public transport. My memories of standing at bus-stops on freezing cold nights, and then having to do my write-up and place it in the sub-editors' basket before I went home, are far clearer than those of the shows I covered. But I do remember, in particular, the lovely little theatre-hall at Bilton, where the most incredibly good productions were staged, against first-class settings – and your critic often finished up by helping to wash the coffee-cups after the show. North Ferriby, Kirkella and many more village drama groups all did sterling work in keeping the live theatre live, and in promoting long-lasting friendships.

One of my blind spots, I must admit, was the arena stage or theatre-in-the-round. For me, the proscenium was an all-time break-through: which of us, having worn nylons, would go back to lisle stockings? The hush as the house-lights dim, then the lifting or parting of the curtain to reveal the set for the first time, as the eyes of the audience are focused upon the raised stage – these, to me, form the quintessential magic, the indispensable psychology of the theatre, whether in lavish building or tiny, rusty, dusty church hall.

Unfortunately for me, the birth of the Janus in 1949 occurred before my career as a theatre reporter had really got going, and I was able to recognise only one of my critiques in the latter part of Stella Sizer-Simpson's story. But I do remember seeing several of the earlier shows, notably *The Eagle Has Two Heads,* and marvelling at the elegant way in which the actresses manoeuvred their huge hooped skirts around that small stage.

Of course, Kevin Carroll, 'Prompter' of the *Hull Daily Mail* and author of *Fires on the Earth,* was a colleague of mine, and we were great friends. I typed the script of the play for him on my old portable at home, and I think that at this distance of time I can reveal that its strong, to me somewhat morbid, Catholic theme grated on my Nonconformist Protestant principles; in fact, I secretly christened it 'The Popish Plot'! But Kevin was the sweetest, sweetest man, as Irish as the Blarney Stone, with a beautiful wife and a lovely family. He used to say that the Janus, in its setting on Hessle Road, in the heart of the then-flourishing fishing industry, reminded him of the Abbey Theatre in Dublin, a theatre as it should be, part of the ordinary working community, with its pubs and chip-shops.

Reading Stella's notes, I realised how excellent was the standard of arts crticism in our local newspapers in those days. How did I ever have the temerity to think that I could begin to match the style and background knowledge of such journalists as David Singleton, Maurice Horspool and the rest? As time went by, we were more and more frequently reminded by the management that our readership was mainly represented by 'Joe Bloggs down Hessle Road'. Full coverage of social events and elegant literary style were increasingly frowned upon. Perhaps, in a way, the management were right. Perhaps the bulk of the population of Hull and the East Riding do lack cultural appreciation and are not theatre-minded. Perhaps that is why the life of the Janus was so tragically short. But it was a pity, for minorities can be important and influential out of all proportion to their numbers, and let us not forget that Hessle Road in the 1950s housed not only Joe Bloggs but the Janus Theatre. After all, our work for the Press is not 'here today and gone tomorrow'; it is preserved in the archives, and referred to by the historians of the future, as witnessed by the many quotes from the newspapers in this book.

My ambition in the beginning had actually been to take part in amateur theatricals, not to write about them, and, apart from our disastrous little enterprise at the 'HDM', I was for a time a member of the illustrious Garret Players. However, they had a nucleus of really first-rank players, and, as they were having great success in competitive festival work, they must naturally have been reluctant to take the risk of bringing along new and untried members for their main productions. I took part in readings, and was invited to help with the business side of the organisation, but, as I was doing office work all day, this seemed too much of a busman's holiday. As I have said, when I started infiltrating into the editorial department, it was mainly through evening jobs, which left me little time for anything else, and, besides, I soon realised that, while there was a desperate shortage of men in the amateur theatre, there was a surplus of women.

So, although I regret that my experience of actually 'treading the boards' was so slight and short-lived, I must acknowledge that, on my way to becoming Woman Editor of the paper, a post I held for 16 years, I did derive a great deal of pleasure and fulfilment from writing about the theatre.

The cast of the comedy-farce, Doctor's Orders, *the first production of the short-lived* Hull Daily Mail *drama group, February, 1952. In the picture are: Kevin Carroll, Jean Morton, Pauline Atkinson, Ron Hopper, Jack herbert, Christine Tarran, Ian Patrick and Barbara Duncanson (later Robinson). Kevin was a sub-editor and 'Prompter' theatre-columnist, Ian was also a 'sub', Ron was from the Accounts Department, Jack was a compositor, and Jean, Pauline, Christine and Barbara were secretaries and office workers. Sadly, the group was not a great success!*
Picture by courtesy of the Hull Daily Mail.

AN ARTS CENTRE IN HULL (AND BEVERLEY)

By Pamela Dellar

ALAN PLATER has already mentioned in his foreword that we tried to set up an Arts Centre for Hull in the 1960s. The ideas for an Arts Centre had been in the air for some time. A pamphlet was published in 1946 by the Citizens Arts League giving detailed plans for a new, multi-purpose Arts Centre, but they suffered the same fate as the Abercrombie Plan, so when Harold Dellar and I left the touring Century Theatre and came to Hull in 1954, the cultural activities were limited and there were few places to meet like-minded people with an interest in the arts.

A notable exception was the Ferens Art Gallery, and I recall the pleasure we experienced on entering the building to see before us a fountain in the centre gallery. Sadly, it was removed in the 1960s. At the New Theatre there was a weekly 'rep' of variable standard, whilst, uniquely, music hall still flourished at the Palace Theatre on Anlaby Road. The City Hall provided a venue for major orchestral concerts.

The amateur theatre seemed to be flourishing, but even here difficulties were being experienced, for the Janus Theatre in Hessle Road was on the point of closure. A new group was just forming at St Mary's, Lowgate; it was called the Company of the Way, and I joined it for their production of James Kirkup's *Candle in the Heavens*, and later became the company's secretary.

In 1964 I was invited by the Rev. Alan Johnston to attend a meeting to discuss an Arts Centre for Hull. This led to the formation of the Hull Arts Centre Appeal Group and I became the secretary – little knowing what I was taking on! Our brief was:

1. To prepare detailed plans for the formation of an Arts Centre in Hull, either:
   a) The Church Institute with extensions to vacant land adjoining, or
   b) A completely new building.
2. To seek assistance from public bodies, industry and individuals and to grant membership to all interested persons.
3. To formulate a deed of constitution to be submitted for approval.
4. To appoint a committee to act on the above.

I sent out numerous circulars to the ever-increasing number of groups and individuals who supported the idea. These were mainly written by Alan Plater, who had also been voted on to the committee, as were Chris

Powell (Chairman), Janet Blackman, and Norman Staveley (Treasurer). Peter Wilson, the architect, and Muriel Crane were co-opted to the committee, and the project was officially launched in October 1964. We published a booklet written by Alan called The Living Arts. In it we outlined our plans – they were very similar to those of the 1946 pamphlet, though at the time I must admit I did not know about that original document. Jenny Lee, the Minister for the Arts, wrote us a letter giving her best wishes; she was 'sure that you are fully in touch with your Local Authorities'. We used the letter as a foreword.

Thereafter, we ran a series of fund-raising activities which helped to keep us in the public eye, but did not raise much money. The events were very varied, and among the most successful was an exhibition and sale of cartoons donated by Abu; this was organised by Nina Kidron. A jazz music programme, Ex Africa, was held in the new Middleton Hall of Hull University, and folk events, always popular, were run by John and Kathy Mitchell.

We continued to hold long meetings in Alan Plater's front room, but by late 1965 we were beginning to lose our momentum and were coming to the conclusion that the large scheme for a new building could not be realised. Our only hope lay in thinking on a smaller scale and we put all our energies into trying to acquire the Church Institute, a gracious building situated next door to the Central Library.

At the time, I was still the secretary of the Company of the Way, which had become a 'Town-and-Gown' group specialising in classics and plays by new writers. Professor Desmond Donovan and his wife, Louise, offered us a rehearsal base in the music room of their Georgian house in Keldgate, Beverley, and it was agreed to run it also as a venue for a mixed programme of arts events. We named it the Keldgate Arts Centre and set about restoring it. We raised funds through an auction, kind supporters each donating 'a treasure from the attic'. Then the floor was sanded, the walls decorated in the colours of the period and the original fireplace was restored. It was very elegant and even had its own separate entrance and foyer.

Although the project was run by the Company of the Way, it became an experimental base for the Arts Centre Group and in 1966 we ran a programme of events over a period of seven or eight months. Friends of Alan Plater rallied round. A group of young writers from Birmingham sent sketches, adding 'We'd like you to put in the programme that the sketches are by Malcolm Bradbury, Jim Duckett and David Lodge'! Henry Livings was a friend and colleague from Century Theatre days. He had gone to work with Joan Littlewood at Theatre Workshop and his play EH! had recently been staged by the Royal Shakespeare Company. He and Alex Glasgow were asked to do a show on 1 May. Alex wrote, '1st May, OK – Red Flags must be worn!' John Arden and Margaretta D'Arcy came

68

over to the St John of Beverley Festival and promised to 'come on to the Keldgate Preview at 9.15. Can you put us up on Saturday night?' We did, and, fortified by late-night bacon and eggs, the writers talked into the small hours of the morning.

Northern writing was flourishing and the drift to the South was resisted in these heady, optimistic days. With the help of Alfred Bradley and Alan Ayckbourn we contacted writers from the popular radio programme, *Northern Drift*, who allowed us to use their material for a show called *Lost up the Creek*. The title was derived from some of the adverse remarks made about the area by the national Press (but not the *Yorkshire Post*) during the famous 'you-shall-have-your-bridge' North Hull by-election.

The manager of the New Theatre was co-operative and provided us with an advance list and contacts for companies which were booked to perform there. This is how we managed to offer an Evening of Opera provided by members of Sadler's Wells Opera with their chorus leader, Hazel Vivienne, while the company was visiting Hull's New Theatre in January 1966. The chorus members loved the opportunity to sing in the pleasant surroundings of the music room and enjoyed the supper that Louise prepared for them afterwards.

Anthony Hedges wrote enthusiastically that 'when I was in Glasgow there was a similar organisation which met in the drawing-room of a large house' – but had we got a piano? A piano was essential! We hadn't, but we hired one for his evening of 'Frothy French Music' during the St John of Beverley Festival.

Professor Edwin Dawes provided a programme of 'Magic and Mystery Through the Ages', and my own recently-formed children's theatre group presented a Chinese folk tale, *The Magic Tea-Kettle*. Louise Donovan, who helped to mount and promote the events, wrote to me irately after this, 'The use of the music room is to cease immediately unless at children's shows there is an adult detailed to control the swarm who go to use *our* lavatory'! There were other understandable grievances as well.

A series of exhibitions was organised by Marcia Tyler, and on one occasion I was called out at 2 a.m. to go and quieten one of their launch parties. I find that artists get very excited when they have an exhibition to launch! This time it had spilled on to the street and the neighbours were complaining. It was beginning to be a strain on my own personal resources.

Then the final blow was struck when Professor Donovan was appointed to a Chair of Geology in London. The house was to be sold. Meetings were held, and at one point Beverley Borough Council seemed distinctly interested. The Town Clerk wrote that they had been 'very surprised to see the excellent progress which had been made at Keldgate'. They finally came to the decision that the Council could not be recommended to purchase Professor Donovan's house 'either in whole or in part' but they offered space at the Mission Hall, the Memorial Hall and the Art Gallery with the possibility of grants for special events.

Donald Campbell and Bertram Wood wrote to the Donovans on behalf of the Keldgate Arts Centre advising them to 'sell your house to the highest bidder. We have all enjoyed working on the project . . . and we have proved that there is a need for an organisation of this kind.' Muriel Crane wrote, 'The people of Beverley (and Hull?) deserve the amenity of such an Arts Centre, subsidised at national and local level on the lines laid down in the Government White Paper, *A Policy for the Arts, 1965*'.

Alan Plater wrote to me of his concern 'that the momentum built up by Keldgate might be lost or at any rate diffused if we simply move back to Square One'. He went on to suggest erecting a tent on Queen's Gardens for a month in the summer and packing it with a series of events. We agreed that we had learned a lot from the Beverley experiment but that our true commitment was to Hull. We paused and reflected . . .

Then things began to happen. Dennis Simms, who had helped us so much at Keldgate, set up a little theatre for the Garret Players in his own house in Westbourne Avenue. Then Alan Johnston reported to the Arts Centre Group that St Stephen's Church Hall could be acquired for a peppercorn rent from the Church Commissioners. Then we received a donation of £2,000 and we were off again! The fund-raising re-started in earnest, and at last the Arts Council took an interest in the project under the *Housing the Arts* programme. There was funding around at last.

By December 1967 Alan was able to write to the committee members:

'One or two things you should know about, but not enough to justify a meeting, not this near the festive season etc.

1. Copy of Arts Council application enclosed, as submitted but *excluding* the plans – though you've probably seen these anyway.
2. Arts Council response. I have had a letter from Mr Linklater of the Drama Section to say that:
   a) The Drama Panel has recommended that the Housing the Arts Committee (which deals with capital grants) "consider sympathetically" our application. Apparently we are asking for a greater *proportion* of the cost than is usual, but there's no harm in asking.
   b) If the Housing the Arts Committee approves our application, the Drama Panel will recommend a grant or guarantee for the first season.
   c) In both cases the amounts will depend on how much the Arts Council itself received for 1968-69 and they won't know this until January – hence it will be February before we get a final decision. Overall, Mr Linklater's letter is encouraging, but naturally he's got to hedge his bets.

3. The Trustees of the church are meeting next week and I am asking Chris and Norman to go along and be business-like on our behalf – with the object of agreeing the terms of a draft lease. The meeting is Wednesday, 20th.
4. I've been contacted by a chap called Mike Leigh of the Royal Shakespeare Company – mid-20s, actor, director, designer, with a lot of experience in schools work – good credentials on paper. He saw an item in *The Guardian* about the Centre and would like to be considered as its first director. Tremendously and genuinely enthusiastic. I'm hoping to see him when I'm in London this week, though, like Mr Linklater, I'll hedge our bets.

That's all. The only overall thing is that, because of the Arts Council delay, our timetable will have to be nudged back a few weeks; but nothing critical.

And a Merry Christmas to all my readers – yours, Alan.'

I met Mike Leigh recently at one of David Edgar's Theatre Conferences in Birmingham. He told me the story of his 'interview' – it still rankled after all these years. He did come up to Hull and was interviewed by one or two people in Alan's front room. Then for some reason he was sent up to the Scarborough Theatre-in-the-Round as well; I think the Arts Council had suggested a link-up. Anyway, when he got to Scarborough, Ken Boden, the theatre manager, knew nothing about it. Mike was furious and caught the first train back to London, never to return. As it turned out, his colleague, Mike Bradwell, came to Hull two years later and set up his new professional theatre company, working in the same improvisational style as Mike Leigh. He called the company Hull Truck. His administrator was Barry Nettleton and one of his trainee directors for a time was Rupert Creed, later director of the Remould Theatre Company. Averil Creed also worked for them and is now the administrator of Remould. So the seeds were sown for decades of professional theatre in Hull, although, of course, we did not know it at the time.

Things went on from strength to strength and on 12 August 1969 the foundation stone for the improved building was laid by Lord Feversham. In 1970 the doors of the Hull Arts Centre were opened for the first time. Janet Blackman became the new chairperson of the committee, and she has described the occasion:

'The glass double doors flew open and a man from a printer's van threw in a bundle of programmes with the words, "I think you need these." Minutes later, flowers followed. This was the opening night in 1970 of one of Britain's first Arts Centres, arguably the first, and this was in Hull – Hull Arts Centre in Spring Street. Behind the local milk factory and opposite the city's mortuary, round the corner from Hull's historic

Speakers' Corner, a town-centre Victorian church hall had been brilliantly and bravely re-built as a centre for the arts.

'A group of local arts enthusiasts and essentially "doers" and performers had brought off one of the most significant ventures at that time for all-comers of all ages to enjoy, to experience, to take part in, to mind and care about theatre, music, dance, painting, photography, poetry and pottery in their own space. This was designed to be a venue, a home for a mixture – more a medley – of professional actors and artists, theatre-in-education specialists, amateur drama groups, individual performers, music nights on Sundays, sitting around with a drink watching, listening, talking, planning. As such, it had unnerved some of the professional money managers: "Make a go of it, and then we'll see about a grant," was the too-ready response from local government bodies and others. Some were more responsive, and national attention was caught by the idea of the Arts Council beginning to put taxpayers' money into local performing arts venues outside London.'

Our director of plays was Barry Hanson, and Rick Welton was our administrator. The opening production was *Don't Build a Bridge, Drain the River*, by Alan Plater, with Barry Rutter playing the lead. Hull Arts Centre Ltd had a magnificent couple of years, but with no local authority support, as all had hoped, it rapidly fell into debt. Janet found herself coping with endless meetings and discussions about funding.

Thankfully, I was no longer the honorary secretary, but I remained on the board. Alan worked tirelessly to present our case in London and to the newly-formed Yorkshire Arts Association, but, without matching funds from local authorities, all hands were tied. There is not room here to describe the agonies and triumphs of that decade from 1972 to 1982. Administrators and directors came and went. Jon Marshall, who really headed the Theatre in Education team, took on a combined administrator-director role in a selfless attempt to save the centre. We were re-named the Humberside Theatre in exchange for a touring commitment in the region and financial support from the new Humberside County Council, but the problems continued.

In 1981, Lincolnshire and Humberside Arts, the regional arts association, threatened to withdraw their financial support and the theatre faced imminent closure. We were saved by the property boom! On behalf of Humberside Theatre Trust, Janet went to the Guildhall to ask if the City Council would be willing to offer a loan secured on the building. She received the impression that her request was anticipated, for the value of the property had increased dramatically over the past few years. A rather neat agreement was reached whereby our City Council grant covered repayments. In exchange, the Council received a majority on the board. From then on, all our meetings were held in the warm elegance of the Guildhall, with Councillor Alice Tulley in the chair and Council officers on hand to give advice. To add to our comfort, we were even given cups of tea and chocolate biscuits! We breathed a sigh of relief; the theatre was saved and Hull City Council at last acknowledged its own home-based professional producing theatre.

In 1982, Hull Truck, who had by now achieved an international reputation, made a successful bid to run the theatre, and moved to Spring Street in April 1983, with Barry Nettleton as administrator. Today, 1996, Hull Truck holds a long lease from Humberside Theatre Trust, who still own the theatre. The Trust is made up of three members of the original board; the others are all City Councillors. It meets annually.

Janet writes: 'Over 20 years later, the theatre remains alive and well, more a theatre than an arts centre now, with a renowned resident playwright-led company. The community arts ingredient is still written into the lease as a recognition of what Humberside Theatre Trust is still all about as a living remnant of the original vibrant and daring Hull Arts Centre Company Ltd.'

Over the years, the theatre has focused on professional theatre, with occasional slots for amateur and visiting companies. It has built a strong reputation which reflects well on Hull and the region. Even so, it, too, has problems in securing adequate support from local authorities, some of whom seem unwilling to recognise the enormous publicity value the company provides for its tourist industry as well as the contribution it makes to the cultural vitality of the region. Hull, like Scarborough with Alan Ayckbourn, now houses one of the country's leading playwrights, John Godber. People ask, 'What is it about this isolated North-Eastern seaboard that produces such unusual theatre?' No-one knows the answer.

But this isn't the Arts Centre of our dreams or of those of the Citizens Arts League of 50 years ago. Looking at Hull today, one sees that some of the aims have been achieved, albeit in a piecemeal fashion. There is now a theatre in Hessle Road, where the Northern Theatre Company opened their little theatre in the 1980s. Their youth theatre has a national reputation, and they provide space for amateurs to perform.

The Library has a very popular film theatre, which attracts support from the British Film Institute. There is a superb, as yet under-used, performance arts space in the extended Ferens Art Gallery. The New Theatre has been partly refurbished, although the back-stage still leaves a lot to be desired, and consequently it is not a favourite booking with the actors. The City Hall still provides a rather uncomfortable venue for major orchestral concerts with chairs set out for the event – is also doubles for such things as afternoon tea-dances. Smaller-scale concerts and chamber music concerts are held in the University's Middleton Hall, a venue with huge potential as a University Arts Centre (it also houses the University Art Collection) but it is under-developed and inadequately publicised. The University also has the Gulbenkian Studio Theatre (the

Donald Roy Theatre); and a number of other studio theatres exist in educational venues. There are no public art galleries for selling art-work although there are some artists' studios in High Street.

A grandly-titled 'Cultural Enterprise Centre' exists in Middleton Street; it is really an old Victorian school. This houses Remould Community Theatre Company, Theatre in Education and the Humberside Dance Agency. There is a dance studio and rehearsal space for the groups. On Northumberland Avenue there is a Community Arts Resource Centre which I developed in the 1980s with the help of a Gulbenkian Foundation grant and which now specialises in media activities. Hull Time Based Arts has a base in Posterngate and concentrates on performance art and installations. Elsewhere in the city popular music flourishes though there is a shortage of rehearsal and recording space for groups; poetry readings are held in smoky rooms of pubs and cafes and comedy venues open and close.

The amateur theatre scene has changed. There are many more little groups who work, almost professionally, in any space they can find. They form and re-form, take off for Edinburgh and are sometimes never seen again. They are innovative, and part of the strange, isolated culture of the City of Hull that is unique, under-funded, underground and insecure. They produce groups like Gill Adams's Big Fish Theatre Company, which led to Gill being given a writer's residency at the National Theatre. But there is the solid core of amateur theatre groups still with no home of their own – the Playgoers, the Chameleon Players, the Avenues Theatre, to name but a few. All the companies in this book have tried to establish a secure base at some time or other and some, like the Playgoers and the Janus, managed to do it. Perhaps a truly bold initiative will bring the groups together to create their own Little Theatre in the city, for, as Sir Ian McKellan said, as visiting Professor in Contemporary Theatre at Oxford, 'Good amateur theatre underpins the professional theatre, and is a prime sign of the appetite of the English for theatre.' The essays in this book provide unique evidence of this.

What else can the future hold? Perhaps Hull's theatres will group together in the Kingston Square area with shared administrative resources. There is also a recognised need for community arts resources throughout the city. But I must admit I look wistfully at the buildings pictured in the 1946 pamphlet – a concert hall in Sweden, a Congress Hall in Switzerland ... Even the waterfront scene is a possibility today – what a superb venue the banks of the Humber could make for a brilliant new concert hall and, incidentally, a centre for Hull's jazz festival and sea-shanty festival, together with a riverside sculpture park, base for community theatre, dance studios, theatre in education, children's theatre, musicians' practice-rooms, artists' studios and shops, restaurants cafés, exhibitions ... !

Ah! Dream on ...   Pamela Dellar, 1996

SOME OTHER MAJOR SOCIETIES

THIS LIST was compiled from responses to a request for information in the *Hull Daily Mail*. It is by no means intended as a comprehensive survey:

The Avenues Theatre Company

THE AVENUES Theatre Company was developed from an evening drama workshop in the 1980s by Pamela Dellar and Lesley Scarr. It now focuses on producing original plays. Various writers within the company enjoy performing work which is both provocative and entertaining without being clichéd. A co-operative company of sorts, anyone can direct, anyone can act, anyone can stage-manage, and this policy has worked well. Purposely keeping membership to approximately 12 maintains tight relationships within the company, making subsequent performances more polished, as the actors are familiar with each other's strengths and weaknesses. For the future? Perhaps to expand the company a little, and, if funding allows, to put on an original play at the Edinburgh Fringe.

Bilton Amateur Dramatic Society

THE ONLY society in Hull with its own theatre. It was founded in 1947 and originally presented its productions in the village hall. In 1953 it moved into the 'social hall' which had been built by Cliff North in the 30's for the men of the village. The first play in the new Bilton 'Theatre' was *Elizabeth I* and the opening ceremony was performed by the actor Richard Ainley and Ida Tether the University extra mural drama lecturer. Cliff North set up a trust which, on his death in 1979, was transferred to the society by his son Keith. Founder members include Margaret and Stan Jackson, Mary Palmer, Biddy Leonard, Muriel Hawkins. This information is supplied by Barbara Jackson.

The Chameleon Players

FOUNDED in 1985, it operates on democratic principles – for example, every member has a say in the choice of play – and with the understanding that experienced members take turn and turn about in performing and giving back-stage assistance. Aiming at three plays a year – a considerable undertaking for a small group – and performing at the Library Theatre or the N.T.C. Studio in Madeley Street, Chameleon have also participated in the 'Peace Play' festival at the Spring Street Theatre, using their own original material, and they have presented a varied programme, with the accent on entertainment – comedies, thrillers and melodramas. While they have entered festivals in the past, they do not feel this to be entirely their metier.

The Electricity Players

FORMED IN 1931 by Mr D. R. Friend, exclusively for members of the Hull Corporation Electricity Department, as it was then, this society has a long history of continuous work, consistently high standards, and a number of festival successes. Wisely not attempting plays outside the range popular with their loyal following, they have maintained their support over the years, and are currently presenting two plays a year, with, in addition, one-act works for festival entries. Before the war, they played at All Saints Parish Hall, Margaret Street, and other church halls. In 1938 they presented *The Strange Case of Blondie White*, and in 1939 *Painted Sparrows*, both at the Royal Institution. After the war, the players used St Augustine's Church Hall in Princes Road, initially for Priestley's *When We Are Married.* Later, the Farmery Hall and St Stephen's Church Hall in Spring Street were tried out. In 1972 the players switched to the Library Theatre, where they still frequently perform. In the early post-war years, the Electricity Authority held their own National Festival, which the Players won in 1960 with a riotous *Sailor, Beware.* With privatisation, the Electricity Authority Festival ceased, as did the Yorkshire Electricity One-Act Festival; but the Electricity Players in Hull continued to support festival work through the British Drama League until its demise, and through the Haltemprice Drama Festival, with both entries and administrative and technical support. Long-standing members Jack and Elma Ray are well-known in the area, having given service to societies such as the Company of the Way, in addition to their commitment to the Electricity Players.

The Elizabethans

AFTER THE CLOSURE of the Janus Theatre in 1954, a small group of the Stella Sizer-Simpson Company commenced work under the title 'The Elizabethans'. Among the founder-members were John and Dennis Chappell, Richard and Ivy Eaves and Trevor and Vivian Tolson. Plays were mounted, in the main, at St Vincent's Hall, Queens Road, and ranged from light entertainment – *Intent to Murder* – to classics such as *She Stoops to Conquer.* A well-remembered highlight was the production of *The Little Hut,* considered at that time a very risqué play for an amateur cast. Vivian Tolson recalls that she ' . . . dared not let her mother come to see it'! Unfortunately, the society closed in the late 1950s when several members of the group left Hull.

Hull Community Theatre

SPECIALISES MAINLY in participation plays for children although other notable productions include a local history promenade play set in the East Riding and called *Only a Man Labouring* and the *Hull Play of Noah* presented for Hull Festival. Many of the present members originally attended the College of Higher Education's large community theatre workshop which was closed by economy cuts in 1979 (See *People Make Plays*, Highgate 1992). Some of them took the name and formed an independent group. Their director and designer was John Munday who died suddenly in 1991. Other founder members include John Alibone, Donald Campbell, John Horsley, Christine Johnson, Wendy Munday, Mick Tite, Lynn White, Christine Wilson.

Malet Lambert Old Students Drama Circle

THIS GROUP, originally the Old Cravonians Drama Circle, based on the Craven Street Secondary School, changed its name when the school became the Malet Lambert High School. Mary Palmer, who holds a complete collection of the programmes for Malet Lambert, identifies the first performance as taking place in 1928, the founding group playing in St Andrew's Church Hall, Abbey Street, and the Presbyterian Hall, Baker Street. From 1933 the re-formed Circle had the use of the new stage at Malet Lambert High School. Except for a short war-time break, two performances a year were given until 1963, when production problems cut this back to an annual presentation. But people were moving away, students of the school no longer remained in Hull when they left, and the continuity was broken. In 1968, the Old Students Drama Circle handed over to the school's Dramatic Society. During their active years, the Circle supported many British Drama League competitions, both in Hull and out-of-town. In 1938 they joined with the Garret Players in a B.B.C. radio presentation. A number of members joined the cast of the Hull Citizens Arts League's Festival of Britain production of *Murder in the Cathedral* in 1951. Joe Palmer, as a Press cutting records, was a moving Thomas, 'utterly absorbed in his role'. With Ida Teather as producer, working freely in various parts of Hull's ancient Holy Trinity Church, and fine costumes designed by Stella Mary Pearce, who created those originally used in Canterbury, the results were memorable.

The Masque Players, 1948 – 1987

THIS GROUP was active in Hull, and well-known for its work in the Haltemprice Drama Festival. Founder-members John and Doris Towse, with Mr and Mrs Edwards and Mrs Woolhouse, started the company 'to promote dramatic art' in their area of Hull, and later through their affiliation to the North Hull Community Centre, and this inter-action continued until 1984. During their history, the Players staged 69 productions for the pleasure of their loyal and regular following, including established favourites such as *Hobson's Choice* and *When We Are Married*, with comedies such as *Goodbye, Mrs Puffin* and an occasional thriller for good measure. Productions were initially in Lonsdale Street, the North Hull Community Centre and Southella Way Church Hall, and later at St Stephen's Church Hall, Spring Street, which saw so many amateur groups pass through before its metamorphosis. Among those who appeared with the Masque Players before moving into the professional theatre are Aline Waites, who was in the B.B.C,'s *Mrs Dale's Diary* and later worked in production; Robert Ornbo, who carved an international name for himself as a lighting designer and technician; and a 16-year-old Richard Green, who features elsewhere in these pages! Sadly, in later years, younger members were not coming forward to take over the work done so thoroughly and for so long by John and Doris Towse and Graham and Joan Walton, and on the deaths of John and Graham the society disbanded. A Masque Players trophy was bequeathed to Haltemprice Drama Festival as a souvenir of their happy association.

The Northern Theatre Company

FOUNDED by Richard Green in 1975,the Northern Theatre Company is now based in its Studio Theatre on Hessle Road. Professionals and amateurs work closely together and the company provides a training base for those moving on to the professional theatre. The full story of the founding of the company, written by Richard Green, is in *People Make Plays*, published by Highgate of Beverley in 1992.

The Phoenix Players 1948 – 1960

THE PHOENIX PLAYERS 'rose from the ashes' of the Drasdo Repertory Company, and, in its first years, Hannchen Drasdo herself, though her health forbade her any other active involvement, served as President. Bridging productions between the two, had been a Sunday supporters' club for the New Theatre staging of *China Bridge* by founder member Sidney Carver, who also wrote *'Tis a Friendly Ghost* for the Drasdo Repertory Company before writing and producing other works under the 'Phoenix' banner. *Comedy Wears a Mask, All for the Love of a Lady, We Twain are Met* (in which Sidney is remembered for a swashbuckling François Villon), *Mother Genevra* and *Royal Adventurer,* all by Sidney Carver, were interspersed with other plays of distinction, such as *The River Line, Venus Observed,* and an amateur premiere of *The Diary of Anne Frank.* Elinor Stark, actress and secretary with the Phoenix, remembers corresponding with Otto Frank, Anne's father, when he requested memorabilia concerning the production for inclusion in the exhibits of the Anne Frank Museum in Amsterdam. *Royal Adventurer* gained a National Playwrights Award for Sidney Carver, and several other awards in a number of drama festivals. A charismatic actor, Sidney, with Elinor Stark, took 'best actor and actress' medals at the 1957 Harrogate Festival. Costumes were a feature of Phoenix productions, their wardrobe mistress, Jayne Williams, having trained in the Covent Garden Opera costume workshops. The Phoenix Players productions were staged, in the main, at the Farmery Hall, but the Y.P.I., George Street, the James Reckitt Institute, and All Saints Hall, Margaret Street, were also used. Sidney's daughter, Stephanie, appeared in a number of Phoenix productions, and is well known today for her work with Hessle Operatic Society. Like her father, she is equally at home whether acting or directing.

The Wilson Line Drama Circle, 1936 – 1970

THIS WAS formed before the war as a branch of the Ellerman's Wilson Line Athletic Club, and acting membership was originally confined to employees of the company, or their relatives, though no such restriction was imposed on the back-stage personnel. This rule was later relaxed, and the Drama Circle, like other societies in the area, used its own players and 'guest' actors to achieve the necessary casts. The post-war re-formation of the Circle stemmed mainly from the enthusiasm and capabilities of Richard Carmichael, the Wilson Line's Assistant Head of Danish Imports, and, on the technical side, Peter Murray, Head of Gothenburg Exports. These two, with the dynamic Jillian Carmichael, formerly an actress with the Janus Theatre, as the Circle's main producer, swept the Circle along with their personalities and energy. Rehearsal room, property store and workshops were made available in 'Sailmakers', a vast breeze-block shed in Bailey's Yard. This enabled members of the company to build and paint the sets which were a feature of Wilson Line productions. This was a facility granted to the Circle by P. G. Staniforth, an Ellerman's Wilson Line Director, who was impressed by the work the Circle had done in an in-the-round award-winning entry in a Scarborough festival, *The Rainmaker. A View from the Bridge* was another Scarborough Festival success. At its height, the Circle performed as many as three plays a year. In 1965, for instance, they staged *Summer of the Seventeenth Doll, Teahouse of the August Moon,* and *The Importance of Being Earnest.* They also ran a Summer School to train the new intake and extend their members' knowledge of drama. A 'Theatre Workshop' style production of compiled material on the theme of 'Love' was one of their co-operative ventures. In 1966, the Circle followed up the Wilson Line's Gothenburg contacts by taking *She Stoops to Conquer* to Oslo. Travelling by the – then new – roll on-roll off ferry, and taking their scenery with them, they stayed at the University of Oslo while presenting five performances of the Goldsmith play at one of the City's most prestigious modern schools. In addition to producing, Jillian Carmichael designed, and, for the most part, made herself, the elaborate 18th-century costumes. A leading actress for the group, the Managing Director's secretary, Gwyneth Brown, a Licentiate of the Royal Academy of Music, who died at a sadly early age, is still remembered for her fine work with this, and other drama groups.

Groups Affiliated to Churches in the Area

AMONG THOSE on record, some in a name only, the following may be regarded as representative:

The Company of the Way

Founded by Frank Glendenning and Muriel Crane in 1955 at St Mary's Church, Lowgate, to present the best religious plays past and contemporary. Later moved to the University. (See *People Make Plays*, Highgate 1992).

Kingston Wesley Methodist Church Drama Group.

This group is to be congratulated on an uninterrupted record of production since its inauguration in 1946 as a feature of the Church's 'Friendship Club', and later, from 1954, as a Drama Group in its own right, with the aim of promoting the fellowship of the Church. Taking part in the 1951-52 Methodist Church (East Hull Circuit) Festival of Music and the Arts, they gained awards under the adjudication of Phyllis Sharrah and later Margaret Burnett for their presentations of *The Distant Drum* and *Legend*. Productions – usually two a year in the early days – went on at the old Queen's Hall in Alfred Gelder Street, now long demolished, and in the Brunswick Methodist Church Hall, as well as in their own church premises. Two of the original members remain with the group. Their current aim: 'Hopefully to carry on for many more years'.

The Potterill Players

Affiliated to the Sutton Methodist Church, the members of this group, founded by Mr and Mrs A. Scruton and Mrs E. Pashby in 1955 with an initial objective of fund-raising, have made a name for themselves in the area with entertainment that can be presented in the Church Hall for their own supporters, and later toured to the many residential homes and centres for the elderly. The interest and enjoyment the group gain from this is rewarding.

St John's Newland-Patruska

Originally the East Hull Congregational Group, founded in the 1950s, they drew away from their source and, on the death of a founder-member, perpetuated her Christian name, 'Pat' in a new title, The Patruska Players. It was an unusual situation, in that the Patruska Players at one point found themselves with a preponderantly male membership, while the St John's Newland Dramatic Society had the more common high percentage of female members. What could be more sensible than to combine? The two names were therefore contracted to the St John Patruska Players, and the society achieved considerable success with productions ranging from religious drama to hilarious pantomime!